SEAFARING under SAIL
The life of the merchant seaman

SEAFARING under SAIL

The life of the merchant seaman

**BASIL GREENHILL
& DENIS STONHAM**
of the National Maritime Museum

NAVAL INSTITUTE PRESS

Dedication
For Flags, in grateful regard *BJG*
For Helen Julia and
Sarah Elizabeth *DSS*

First published in 1981

Published and distributed in the United States of America
and Canada by the Naval Institute Press, Annapolis,
Maryland 21402.

Library of Congress Catalog Card No: 81-83483

ISBN 0-87021-876-X

Printed in Great Britain

The
CONTENTS

The INTRODUCTION

'When men come to like a sea-life, they are not fit to live on land . . .
Men go to sea, before they know the unhappiness of that way of life; and when they have come to know it,
they cannot escape from it, because it is then too late to choose another profession . . .'

This quotation, from the aphoristic Dr Samuel Johnson and dating from 1776, identifies succinctly some of the main characteristics of the seaman's life, several of which persisted even after the steamship enabled the sailor to enjoy a more regulated, less sequestered life. The steam engine, once reliable and economical in use—that is, after 1865—released the mariner from dependence on wind and current and enabled him to predict accurately his date of arrival in any port in the world. Calms no longer impeded his progress, leaving his ship wallowing on a smooth sea. Heavy weather had less influence over the steamship, which carried within it its own motive power. The life of the sailing ship seaman had been and remained very different.

Frequently he would be away from his home for three years or more, three years being the usual length of service to which the seaman assented when signing the Agreement and Account of Crew at the beginning of a voyage in a big deep-sea vessel. Quite often during that time a ship would not touch a 'home', or European, port and the seaman would be signed off the ship's Articles—or desert—in a foreign port, maybe on the other side of the world. During the course of a voyage he would often be at sea for passages of two or three months without touching at a port. Sometimes, in cases of exceptional weather conditions, the duration of a passage could be extended considerably as in the case of the barque *Lalla Rookh,* built in 1876, which on March 21 1905 sailed from Brisbane, bound for Falmouth with a cargo of wheat. She reached the latter port on October 7. Basil Lubbock records in *The Last of the Windjammers* that she was 100 days from Brisbane to Cape Horn after a severe beating in storm conditions, and on her run up the Atlantic became short of provisions, having to dip into the cargo for food. Posted missing at Lloyd's, the insurance claim on her assumed loss had been settled when she arrived at Falmouth, 199 days from Brisbane.

Another long passage without intermediate landfall was experienced by the steel ship *Denbigh Castle* which sailed from Cardiff for the west coast of South America on October 9 1908 and, failing to beat round the Horn, bore away eastwards arriving at Fremantle, for stores, in June 1909.

The longest voyage undertaken by a merchant sailing ship, although in this case lengthy periods were spent in port repairing, was probably that of the British ship *Garthwray* which cleared from Grangemouth with a cargo of coal for Iquique on July 15 1922. During a passage which lasted 559 days she was twice damaged in attempting to round the Horn, repairing first at Montevideo, than at Cape Town before her master, like the master of the *Denbigh Castle,* decided to go east-about rather than persist with the attempt. Her cargo was discharged at Iquique more than 18 months after it was loaded. Ballast was taken on board and the *Garthwray* sailed for Talcahuano for a homeward cargo of grain but did not arrive, being wrecked en route. Voyages such as these were rare but passages prolonged by stress of weather (and of course periods of exceptional calm) were common.

The segregation of the merchant seaman in sail from society, which was the consequence of long voyages, inevitably set him aside from the land community and imbued him with quite distinct values and an outlook on life alien to that of the landsman. For months he was isolated from the rest of mankind and all womankind in a community comprising a dozen or so inmates of the forecastle, where he lived, and his superiors, the much smaller number of officers who were accommodated aft. A parallel situation ashore, in which men voluntarily immured themselves in such a closed, isolated community, could only be found in the more rigorously cloistered monastic orders. Johnson saw this and recognised that men so long away from shore-life, living for long periods in an environment alien to the rest of society, would inevitably develop standards unlike those of their fellows ashore, making them appear uncouth, inept and out of touch when on land. He was right and to the present day the sailor has remained to a degree a man apart.

Boswell reports that Johnson often enlarged upon the wretchedness of a sea-life, describing a ship as 'worse than a jail'. 'No man', he says, 'will be a sailor who has contrivance enough to get himself into jail; for being in a ship is being in jail, with the chance of being drowned . . . A man in jail has more room, better food and commonly better company.' Johnson, writing this in 1759, would have had little reason to change his opinion of the life under sail more than a century later. The forecastle of the deep-water, square-rigger was often damp, unheated and sometimes it could be a floating slum. In a small space under the forecastle head, right in the bows of the ship, or at best in a deckhouse in the neighbourhood of the foremast, would live maybe twelve or so men. Food prepared within the limits of a sparse, monotonous allowance, would be brought forward from the galley amidships and, in the earlier part of the period covered by this book, eaten by balancing the plate on knees or seachest. In such conditions a crew had to learn to get along together.

Johnson's realisation that men adopted the sea as a career before they were aware of the hardships involved, finding that it was impossible to escape from once the true nature of the life had revealed itself, or because their circumstances offered no other possible choice, was still as true in the 19th century as in the 18th. Employment conditions and opportunities ashore naturally affected recruitment into the British merchant shipping industry during the 19th century and there can be no doubt that large numbers of men went to sea through necessity rather than inclination when job prospects in their locality on shore were poor or non-existent. The peculiar nature of the seaman's skills did, however, render him unsuited for employment in many jobs ashore should he wish to leave the sea. Unless he were to gain employment as a rigger, or maybe a caulker, in a shipyard, his time at sea would be of little benefit to him in any shorebased work. Thus the sailor was obliged to return to sea where his skill would ensure an existence which, albeit hazardous, uncomfortable and ill-paid, had a degree of financial security attached to it. Long voyages and the resultant isolation from his home community put the sailor quite out of touch with the situation at home and he would have little opportunity to seek work ashore at the end of his voyage before his wages ran out and he was forced to seek a ship.

Since conditions at sea in the 19th century were so very different from those enjoyed by the merchant seaman of today, and indeed so totally unlike anything which would be accepted today, ashore or afloat, perhaps histories of the last century of merchant shipping have tended to concentrate too much on the unsatisfactory nature of some aspects of working conditions at sea. It was undoubtedly a hard life, possibly harder and more dangerous than that associated with any major industry ashore, for even the miner was able to be with his family each day, faced rather a smaller risk of death and had perhaps better food than the sailor. The merchant seaman was away from his wife and children (if such he ever had) for months at a time. The landsman, although he might live in crowded, insanitary conditions, could seek solitude and privacy if he wished; the seaman was limited to the confines of the ship's deck and his forecastle, which was always occupied by the watch below. Working conditions unacceptable today were, of course, common during the Victorian and Edwardian eras, but right up until the last British square-rigger left the sea at the beginning of the second quarter of the 20th century, the seamen worked not less than 84 hours per week and rarely more than four hours' sleep at a time.

Nevertheless, at a time in which what to us would seem great hardships were being endured by British industrial workers as a whole, perhaps undue emphasis has been given to the harshness and discomfort of life at sea under sail. We need to attempt to view the seaman's existence through 19th century eyes, bearing in mind contemporary social mores and attitudes.

John Everett, the marine artist, made several voyages in square-rigged ships, his first in the *Iquique* between May 1898 and April 1899. Although beginning this voyage as a passenger, being signed on as an Ordinary Seaman at one shilling per month, Everett worked with the crew and at the end of the voyage was offered the position of third mate, which he refused. His *Journal* reveals much of the life and conditions aboard a large sailing merchantman of the time, and regarding the character of the 'shellback', or merchant seaman in sail, of the time he has this to say:

'The books I read about the sea stress the terrible hardships the sailor had to put up with—wet through for weeks together, the terrible food, the damp places he lived in, working night and day, and a miserable wage. You must remember that they went of their own accord. They were not forced to go. They growled and grumbled the whole time—used to say "put me behind a mountain where I can never see the sea", or "when I get paid off, I shall take an oar and walk into the country. When I get to a place where they say 'what is that?'—that's the place for me!" If you got them a good job ashore they wouldn't stick it—"Oh the hell with this job!"—and back they went. You must remember they were mostly young, in splendid condition. There was a sense of adventure about the life in sail. The hard physical work was an outlet for their energies . . . The hardships they went through were made a joke of. If you got washed into the lee scuppers, wet through in icy water, everybody roared with laughter. To people ashore the things they put up with were terrible hardships . . . It was a man's life in sail.

'With regard to money, they had no sense of money. They were like children. For months together they wanted no money. If you paid them £3 a month or £20 a month, it made no difference to them. No matter what they were paid off with they got rid of it, or it was stolen from them. In fact the man who got rid of his pay the quickest boasted about it and was a sort of hero in the fo'c'sle. They had no possessions. Their only ambition was to get drunk and have a woman. They could buy the few

things they wanted from the Old Man—he usually had a slop chest. And in a sense they didn't have to pay for it. It was deducted from their pay at the end of the month, but no money passed. And if you were gloriously drunk and didn't remember anything you did for the few days you were ashore, it didn't matter. The hardships they went through were confined to certain latitudes. For months they basked in glorious sunshine, with practically nothing on, slept out on deck in those wonderful tropical moonlight, or starlight nights. I've slept for two months in a cot on deck. The food may have been bad and badly cooked, but you had such an appetite you could eat anything and enjoy it. They didn't have to get it or buy it. It was provided for them. They had no worries of bills, rates or Mr Bloodsucker the income tax collector. Oh, it certainly had its advantages. A long passage made no difference to them—more days, more dollars.'

The image generated by Everett's description of these men is of an almost feckless, irresponsible group looking only to sensual pleasure at the end of a hard voyage. If they did seem to a landsman like children it was because the life which they led was remote from the considerations and responsibilities which burdened the shore-dweller. No money was required on board so, as long as there was sufficient left at the end of the voyage to have a spree, that could be dispensed with as something worthy of consideration. There are stories of seamen in Liverpool and elsewhere giving away their money to passers-by on the eve of sailing since, aboard ship, it was an unnecessary encumbrance and worry.

In an age which is increasingly unsure of the future, the simple and ingenuous approach of the crew described could seem almost admirable.

This book attempts to throw some light on to the realities of the life of the deep-water merchant sailing ship seaman. The photographs used have been selected to present the latter-day crews of these vessels, both at work aboard ship and in occasional moments of relaxation. The captions amplify and describe the pictures.

Aboard these ships the crews frequently lived in quarters which today would be considered intolerable, their diet was poor and their work hard and dangerous. Yet the ships were a magnificent sight when under sail on a fine day in a stiff breeze and more than one writer has expressed the opinion that the sailing ship under sail was among the most exciting spectacles it was ever possible to see. In good weather the crew's existence could approach the idyllic; with little heavy work to be done and long days of hot, fine weather, the ship's community could enjoy a period, sometimes of weeks at a time, when no disturbing influence from the outside world impinged on the tranquillity of the ship—but only in fine weather latitudes. Miseries of cold and damp to be endured, the indifferent food and cramped accommodation were the other part of the life.

Part One of this book gives a brief introduction to the most common rigs to be found in late 19th century sailing vessels. Masting and rigging is a complex and technical subject to do justice to which requires a full book. A number have been written, of which the most relevant to the period under review is Harold Underhill's *Masting and Rigging—the clipper ship and ocean carrier*. In the compass of the nine photographs of Part One of this book it has, however, been possible to describe the basic characteristics of each of the major rigs to be found on the oceans in the late 19th century. In descending order of size from the ship and the four-masted barque, the most common of the rigs of deep-sea vessels, each rig down to the two-masted schooner and the brigantine is defined and illustrated.

The gradual evolution of the large merchant sailing ship, from the deep, round-bowed wooden vessel of some 500 tons gross in the 1840s to the big, steel, sailing bulk-carrier of the 1890s, four-masted, powerfully rigged and measuring two or three thousand tons gross, is described in Part Two. The development of the steamship to a point of economic and technical proficiency in the 1860s had a profound influence on the design of the sailing ship, prompting refinement and a deeper concern with the performance and cargo capacity of the wind-driven vessel. Although the inevitable eventual decline of the big deep-sea merchant sailing vessel was established from as early as 1865 when the steam compound engine was first used successfully at sea on a long voyage, and her extinction made certain by the development of the triple-expansion engine in the early 1880s, the sailing ship continued to evolve for another generation.

There was no point at which the advance of the steamship stifled innovation in the design of the more traditional vessel; the very opposite occurred and the increasing numbers of steam-powered vessels appearing on the world's trade routes served to stimulate both builders and owners of sailing ships to produce vessels able to specialise in a number of trades, principally those involving bulk cargoes. Thus, latterly, these ships developed in response to the nature of the trades in which they worked once the steamer had captured the more lucrative trades. Cargo capacity became the main criteria, for the last of the sailing ships carried low-value cargoes in bulk; the ores, grain, nitrates and lumber which were less attractive to the steamship owner. These vessels have been described as a compromise—manoeuvrability being sacrificed in the cause of deadweight capacity. Their crews probably found the ships no harder to work than ships of a half century earlier, the basic principles of rigging being similar in both cases. But, in the name of economy, the number of men carried as crew shrank appreciably over the period, refinements in gear and rigging being evolved to ease the toil of setting, trimming and furling the huge square sails.

The central theme of this book is the merchant seaman in sail and his life and this is described in Part Three, by far the largest section of the book and to which the other parts are complementary. The photographs in this part of the book are all from the latter part of the 19th century and from the 20th century, for pictures of seamen at work are rare indeed from the 1870s and earlier for reasons which will be explained. Nevertheless, these photographs give a good impression of the sailor's lot, the story centering upon four ships: the four-masted barque *Port Jackson* of 1882, the barque *Garthsnaid* of 1892 and the four-masted barques *Medway* and *Passat* of 1902 and 1911 respectively. Each of these vessels was British except the last named which was one of Gustaf Erikson's fleet sailing from the Åland Islands in the Gulf of Bothnia under the Finnish flag.

In addition to the photographs taken on board these ships, a selection of pictures taken aboard a variety of other vessels has been introduced to complement and expand the theme. In this way it has been possible to provide as comprehensive and clear impression of the sailor himself, his working conditions and environment as photographic limitations allow. Many of these photographs are well documented and in some cases this has allowed the accompanying captions to describe them in detail.

Photographs of the activities of the seaman ashore are, not surprisingly, exceedingly rare. The establishments in the dock area where ship's crews tended to congregate were, very often, not those inhabited by people likely to understand or welcome the presence of a camera. Sadly, there are almost no photographs of the boisterous pubs, bars and dance-halls patronised by the deep-water sailorman around the world. In most major ports there came to be established separate quarters of the town which devoted part, if not all, of their commercial enterprise to the entertainment, diversion (and quite frequently fleecing) of the crews from the ships in port. Although popular with the seaman, few of the sailor-haunts in these areas were in any way whatever concerned with his moral, spiritual or financial welfare. Lurid tales are told of many of these sailor-towns, of the robbings and fights which were nightly occurrences in the bars and dives, of the crimping establishments which traded in ships' crews, even drugging the men and putting them insensible aboard outward-bound vessels. Photographs of ten ports familiar to the square-rigger sailor, some of which had notorious sailors' quarters, are featured in Part Four.

Seafaring has always been a hazardous occupation. The wooden merchant sailing ship—especially the fast vessel—was probably the most dangerous vehicle ever used regularly on a large scale. The late big steel vessels were less inherently dangerous but still subject to casualties in great numbers, and during the 19th century what now seem appalling losses among ships and men were suffered each year. Even today large, well-found vessels occasionally go missing at sea with little or no clue to their fate, but during the last century very many men were lost in ships which simply disappeared between ports, being overwhelmed by stress of weather, foundering after springing a leak or even catching fire and burning to the waterline. Casualties such as these, together with collisions, strandings and all other marine hazards, accounted for the total loss of more than one hundred British registered sailing vessels engaged on ocean passages each year in the late 1870s and early 1880s. During the year 1876-77, 201 such vessels were lost, taking with them 1,639 men. Seven years later, during 1883-84, 145 vessels came to grief involving a loss of 1,220 lives. These figures are quite apart from the very high losses incurred in the coastal trade and fishing fleet and among steamships. Representative incidents portraying the variety of perils with which the sailing ship seaman was faced are illustrated and described in Part Five.

The progress of the merchant sailing ship and her men from the mid-19th century, when steam had posed no serious challenge and vessels under sail outnumbered powered ships by more than twenty times, to the very end when sailing ship owners were making small profits with vessels which represented a relatively small investment, is our concern in this book. From the time that the first compound-engined steamship made a long ocean voyage in the 1860s, the trades which had been those of the square-rigged ship unchallenged began to pass more and more to the steam vessel. The utmost economy of operation had to be rigorously exercised if sail was to offer a service to the shipper which would be attractive in terms of cost when compared with the faster, more dependable steamer. New rigs had to be tried in an attempt to reduce manning costs and labour-saving devices exploited further to reduce the burden of work falling to a small crew. Gradually, however, the steamship became economical enough in operation to compete in all but a very few of the world's trades. Part Six describes some of the characteristic features of the last days of sail, taking the story through many of these developments and describing two of the very last fleets of large sailing vessels left in trade, the curtain closing with the remarkable enterprise established and controlled by Gustaf Erikson, a former yeoman-shipmaster from Åland.

The photograph is a powerful medium with which to present this appraisal of the life of the sailing-ship seaman. It is immediate in evoking a response yet is capable, at a deeper level, of almost infinite interpretation in its complexity of image. A photograph such as Plate 39, for example, showing the barque *Garthsnaid* rolling heavily to port in a gale, not only provokes an instant awareness of the discomforts to be endured by the crew of the ship in bad weather but, on closer inspection, reveals much fine detail. In this respect photographs, as documents of history, are unique. Other sources, among which might be numbered paintings and drawings, the large majority of written records including diaries, autobiographies and journals and even the oral recordings which increasingly are finding their way into national archives, are all the products, to varying degrees, of human fallibility, prejudice and hence selection.

It may be argued, however, that photographs are less vulnerable to subjectivity than almost any other historical source, for a photographer, unlike a writer, artist, diarist or chronicler, is not to any great extent in control of his medium. Whilst photographs cannot be entirely free from subjective elements, inasmuch as the photographer is at liberty to choose the composition of his picture and may position himself when making the exposure, or crop the resultant print in order to eliminate elements which may compromise his desired purpose, they retain more of an incident than can other forms of historical evidence. Study of a photograph allows us to view a scene or incident almost as in life. We are able to make much the same judgements and form similar opinions, as we might had we actually been present to witness the event—in fact better judgement, pre-considered, in detachment and at leisure. It is to photographs that we can go for proof and confirmation (or otherwise) of facts drawn from other, more conventional, sources. These frozen moments of history are indeed a glimpse into the past allowing us, subject to availability of sufficient suitable photographic images, to draw our own conclusions and make our own interpretations largely free from the influence of exterior bias.

It is fortunate that so many images relating to the large, deep-sea sailing ship have survived, enabling a comprehensive photographic account of the ships and their crews to be compiled. It was not until the 1880s, however, that the photographic process became generally accessible to all. In 1879 George Eastman patented a machine for coating dry plates and it was the introduction of these small glass photographic plates, purchased ready sensitised, which increased the practicability of amateurs embracing photography without necessarily becoming involved in complex chemical processes. The wet-plate photographic process which preceded this innovation required the glass plates to be coated with the light-sensitive emulsion immediately before the exposure was to be made, for the emulsion rapidly lost its sensitivity in drying. The disadvantage of this process, of course, although it produced negatives of splendid clarity and detail, was that all the paraphernalia of the darkroom had to be on hand wherever the exposure was to be made, involving the transport of much equipment, including camera and tripod, the plates and chemicals for sensitising, developing and fixing them, plus a dark tent in which to apply the emulsion to the plates. A long exposure time also rendered this process unsuitable for recording any event where much movement was taking place. Thus few photographs of shipboard scenes taken before the 1880s exist.

But once the small hand-held camera, using dry-plates requiring only a relatively short exposure time, appeared, the photographic process became a commonplace. Negatives once exposed could be kept in light-tight conditions for some time before being passed to a processer for developing and printing. In many cases these negatives were developed, fixed and printed aboard ships on passage, a case in point being the photographs of the four-masted barque *Port Jackson* in Part Three of this book. It will be seen, from Plate 28, that photographs could also be taken in the relative gloom of the ship's accommodation with little difficulty. The virtual absence of any photographs of the crew's accommodation forward or in the half-deck at this time can be explained by the very cramped nature of these quarters which allowed the photographer little room or opportunity to make a worthwhile picture and by the fact that these were the men's private living quarters.

Ten years after the machine for coating dry-plates had been patented, Eastman and his associates produced a satisfactory transparent celluloid negative film coated with a gelatine emulsion for their new Kodak camera. With the comprehensive developing and printing service which he had set up, Eastman then felt justified to say that his Kodak camera could be operated by anyone 'who has sufficient intelligence to point a box straight and press a button'. This camera and those like it were usually of the folding, bellows type and could be carried easily in the hand and slipped into the pocket when not in use. Unlike the earlier plate cameras the negative did not need to be removed once each exposure had been made but the film simply wound on to the next frame, the whole film being taken from the camera in a tightly wound roll once all frames had been exposed.

Any passenger, officer or even seaman aboard ship could, with one of these roll-film cameras, make his own pictures with the minimum of inconvenience to himself and the least disruption to the work of the ship. Providing not too much water was blowing about on deck, a camera could be tucked away in a convenient spot and retrieved to capture an interesting moment on film if and when an opportunity arose.

The photographs of the barque *Garthsnaid,* also to be found in Part Three, are examples of pictures made in just this way. The prints reproduced here are all from small film negatives which were most probably taken by the barque's second officer, Mr Turner. It seems that Mr Turner had his camera to hand throughout a voyage from Iquique to Delagoa Bay in 1919 and used it to good effect. Numbered amongst these negatives are some of the very best photographs ever taken showing a big merchant sailing vessel at sea in heavy weather.

The majority of the negatives from which the photographs in this book have been reproduced have been selected from the 20,000 which once formed part of the Nautical Photo Agency and which were presented to the National Maritime Museum in December 1966. There can be no doubt that it is due to the Nautical Photo Agency that a large number of fine photographs depicting very many aspects of man's use of the sea for purposes of trade, war and pleasure, have survived. The Agency was founded in 1926 by Captain Fred C. Poyser and the marine journalist Frank Bowen.

Captain Poyser had always had an intense interest in the sea, particularly in sailing ships, and served his time in the three-masted barque *Inverness,* owned by George Milne & Company, after training in the Merchant Navy Cadet School *Conway.* From the beginning of his career he began to accumulate sailing ship negatives and it is said that after he had gone into steamships he was sometimes able to persuade his captains to alter course when a sailing vessel was sighted, in order that he might photograph her. Fred Poyser saw the value of the photograph in preserving the memory of the sailing merchantman which was, by the end of the First World War when he came ashore, fast disappearing from the oceans.

Together with Frank Bowen, Captain Poyser conceived the idea of establishing a central archive of maritime photographs which would be of use to historians, the news media and to collectors. Once the Agency had been set up and announced, the great number of friends and acquaintances which both Bowen and Poyser had throughout the world began to give or lend their negatives to the enterprise. One of these men was James Randall, examples of whose work are included in this book (see Plates 69, 70 and 72).

Gradually the Agency grew until it comprised tens of thousands of negatives, some originals and some copies of fading prints thus preserved. Captain Poyser ran the Agency until his death, at the age of 71, in 1960. Following Captain Poyser's death the Nautical Photo Agency was gradually wound down by his widow Mrs Grace Poyser, negatives being returned to those who had loaned material to the Agency. Six years later the remaining 20,000 negatives of both steamships and sailing vessels, together with photographs of related subjects, were presented as a magnificent gift to the National Maritime Museum.

The Nautical Photo Agency was an example of the unique interest and value of the photograph being recognised long before the photographic image was regarded as being of anything but inconsequential and ephemeral interest. It is only relatively recently that the historian has accepted the photograph as being worthy of his attention and of use to him as source material. The National Maritime Museum, aided by the Society for Nautical Research, was a pioneer in recognising the historic value of photographs and in establishing an archive of historic photographs. Since its inception in 1947 this archive has grown until today it comprises some half a million images from the earliest days of photography to the present. All of the photographs in this book have been drawn from this vast treasure trove. The use of this material thus allows us not only to present an account of the last century of the seamen who spent their lives in deep-water merchant sailing ships but to demonstrate the unique qualities and worth of the photograph in the relating of this theme. Perhaps the world of the merchant sailing ship, a cloistered, closed community having little contact with society ashore, only imperfectly known to its contemporaries and now so remote from our own experience, is one of the best examples which could be chosen to show the documentary value of the photograph in developing a empathetic insight into a remote area of man's past experience.

Thanks are due to Alan Viner and Campbell McMurray of the National Maritime Museum and to Miss Patricia O'Driscoll for their advice and assistance in the preparation of this book.

13

The RIGS

Plate 1 (Below left)

The most common rigs carried by deep-sea sailing ships in the 19th century were those of the ship and the barque. Here is the large iron ship *Glenalvon* of 1888. It will be seen that she has three masts and that each mast is square-rigged, that is, each carries yards across it from which the sails are set. To qualify for the description 'ship-rigged' each of the three, or more, masts of a vessel had to be rigged in this way. The *Glenalvon* was among the larger of the vessels to carry this rig, being of more than 2,000 tons gross, and although seen here in very light airs was a very fast ship. On one occasion she covered 1,800 miles in five days whilst on passage from Philadelphia to Kobe. Three-masted cargo-carrying sailing ships continued to be given this rig into the 1880s but after this decade new vessels tended to be barque- or four-mast barque-rigged.

Plate 2 (Below)

Altogether throughout the 19th century a very large number of three-masted ships were built. From the mid-1870s onward some 50 or so four-masted ships were launched, but only one five-master with this rig was ever built. This photograph shows that vessel, the *Preussen,* built in Germany in 1902 for the famous shipowning company of Ferdinand Laeisz, and measuring 5,081 tons gross. Despite the fact that the *Preussen* was not the largest sailing vessel ever built, her dimensions are impressive. The height of her mainmast was 223 ft from keel to truck and she had a sail area of 50,000 ft^2. Like all very big sailing vessels she proved difficult to handle and she met an untimely end when in 1910, following a collision, she went aground under the South Foreland and broke her back.

The barque, popular throughout the first three-quarters of the 19th century, became even more common in the last decades, largely for economic reasons. It will be seen from this photograph of the barque *Willscott* of 1896 that the rig is much the same as that of the ship except that the aftermost, or mizzen, mast is not square-rigged but sets a fore-and-aft sail on gaff and boom. In the photograph the sail can be seen brailed in against the mast. Increasing competition from steamships induced sailing ship owners to reduce every expense possible and, in an attempt to minimise the number of crew aboard their vessels, many shipowners removed the mizzen yards from their ship-rigged vessels, so reducing them to barque rig with a consequent reduction in the amount of sail handling necessary. The *Willscott*, seen here new from her builders, has a bald-headed rig, that is to say she crosses no yards above her double topgallants.

Plate 4 (Below)

As competition for freights with triple-expansion-engine steamships intensified in the 1880s, it became imperative to take advantage of developing technology and increase the deadweight, or carrying, capacity of sailing vessels. Ships and barques began to be built to increasingly greater dimensions, frequently exceeding the 2,500-ton gross mark, and the three-masted rig ceased to be adequate. The big, steel four-masted barque such as the one in this photograph, the American *Star of Greenland,* built at Glasgow in 1892 as the *Hawaiian Isles,* began to become very popular with shipowners. The rig is the same as that of the ship but the hull is longer and a fourth, gaff-rigged, mast is added. In the case of the four-masted barque the aftermost mast is known as the jigger and the square-rigged masts as the fore, main and mizzen.

Plate 5 (Left)

With just two masts, both square-rigged, this is the brig *Ellen Simpson,* built at Sunderland in 1847. It can be seen that her masts and rigging are similar to those of a ship, but whereas a ship must have a minimum of three square-rigged masts in order to be so described, a brig has only two with a large spanker sail set abaft the aftermost, the mainmast. A feature to be seen in this photograph is the bentinck boom to which the foot of the foresail was attached. In the photograph this boom can be seen lying across the brig between the bowsprit and the foremast. Its purpose was to help control the foot of the foresail when putting the brig about, or trimming the sail when sailing on the wind, so eliminating a lot of the running rigging found on the foresails of larger vessels.

Plate 6 (Above)

The barquentine developed in the 1830s, apparently more or less simultaneously in Nova Scotia and in North Germany, and small barquentines were used in many trades all over the world. In the 1880s and

after, in the face of increasing competition from steamships in previously traditional sailing ship trades, it was important that every saving in expenditure should be made and the rig became very popular for medium-sized vessels, especially in North America. The rig combines elements of both square and fore-and-aft rigs but without the expense of fitting and manning more than one square-rigged mast; the main driving force in the barquentine coming from the large sails set schooner fashion on gaffs and booms. The lower sails could be handled from the deck with the aid of a steam donkey engine without the necessity to go aloft as in the case of the square-rigged foremast, although the handling of the large gaff topsail, as with those of the big schooners, was perhaps the most difficult work aloft the crews of any sailing vessels were ever called upon to perform. This vessel, the *Echo,* built in Oregon in 1896, was of 707 tons gross but carried a crew of only nine men. A ship-rigged vessel of comparable tonnage might be expected to have a crew of around 14. In a barquentine the foremast is always square-rigged and the two or more additional masts always rigged fore-and-aft. Two barquentines with as many as six masts have existed; one of them, the American *E.R. Sterling,* was one of the most successful 20th century sailing vessels.

Plate 7

The deep-sea schooner reached its fullest development in the great wooden four-, five- and six-masters built on both seaboards of North America. In Britain the rig was confined, largely, to small vessels with two or three masts nearly always crossing one or two yards on the foremast. This vessel, the steel schooner *Honolulu,* is a rarity, for although built in the American tradition she was launched from the Port Glasgow shipyard of Robert Duncan and Company Ltd in 1896. She is rigged Pacific Coast style without topmasts or gaff topsails. In the latter day American sense the schooner is a vessel of two or more masts each rigged with fore-and-aft sails and carrying no square sails at all. Each of the huge sails shown in this photograph could be handled from the deck, using steam-driven winches, with a consequent saving in the number of crew required. Very large vessels were able to carry schooner rig; the biggest being the 5,218-tons gross *Thomas W. Lawson,* built in 1902 and rigged with seven masts. The *Honolulu* was of 1,080 tons gross and was 206 ft long. She is flying the flag of Hawaii.

Plate 8 (Above)

This vessel is the schooner *Duchess,* built at Connah's Quay on the River Dee in 1878. It will be remembered that a schooner is a vessel of two or more masts, each of which is fore-and-aft rigged, and the *Duchess* complies with that rule. In addition, however, she carries square sails on her fore topmast with a running square sail set from the lower yard. These topsails are characteristic of the British schooner and were not commonly set on later schooners built in North America. Both two- and three-masted topsail schooners were numerous around the British coast from the middle of the 19th century but most were diminutive compared with the huge American-built schooners. Many of these small vessels made long ocean voyages and some, especially those in the Mediterranean and Azores fruit trades, were very fast vessels indeed. The *Duchess,* seen here under sail off Rame Head, was still at work in the early 1930s.

Plate 9 (Below)

In the sense that the term 'brigantine' was most commonly understood in Britain in the latter part of the 19th century, it describes a vessel having a fully square-rigged foremast and a fore-and-aft rigged mainmast. In comparing this photograph of the brigantine *Gilpin* with the previous one of the schooner *Duchess,* the most noticeable difference between the rigs is the absence in the former of the large, fore-and-aft rigged foresail set by the schooner. The *Gilpin,* in its stead, sets a full suit of staysails between her fore and main masts. Further, the brigantine sets course, topsails and topgallantsails, and even royals, on her foremast (which is in three parts) whereas the schooner, normally, only crosses yards on her fore topmast and her foremast is in only two parts. Many of these small ships were engaged in similar deep-sea trades to the equally small schooners in the 1860s and 1870s and a large number of them were built in the maritime provinces of Canada— especially in Prince Edward Island—and sold to British owners. The *Gilpin,* shown here setting her mainsail as she leaves Ramsgate Harbour, was one of these vessels, having been completed in Prince Edward Island late in 1869.

The EVOLUTION OF THE MERCHANT SAILING SHIP

Until the middle of the 19th century, progress in the development of the merchant sailing ship was extremely slow. The vessel in this photograph is the barque *William Miles,* built at Bristol in 1816. Her very full lines and the almost flat face which her bows present to the sea are characteristic of sailing ships of her time and, indeed, of vessels until the 1860s. Not until then did the evolution of the steamship stimulate any serious competition to the sailing ship on the world's trade routes. Consequently, until this time, the appearance of the sailing ship changed little from that of the previous century. In addition, the requirement to convoy merchantmen during the long Napoleonic Wars further repressed any need to make changes in hull form which might have led to faster ships. Cargo capacity, not speed, was of overriding importance. Further, ships such as the *William Miles* were required to be able to sit upright in ports which dried out at low tides, for not many seaports at that time had wet docks which could keep ships afloat independent of the tides. They were, therefore, flat-bottomed and box-sectioned amidships. This latter characteristic can be appreciated in the case of the *William Miles* in spite of the fact that in this photograph she is shown lying afloat.

Another factor which contributed significantly to the design and appearance of the early 19th century sailing merchantman was the tonnage law in force between 1773 and 1836, but which had an influence reaching far beyond that date. This act specified a formula from which could be established a tonnage for each vessel. From this figure could be calculated the harbour and pilot dues incurred by a ship. It was, however, worked out by measuring only the length and breadth of the ship. A figure representing the depth of hold was arrived at by calculation, but the actual depth was not measured. Because of this it became customary to build very deep ships with a cargo capacity greater than less deep vessels of the same length and breadth but of no greater registered tonnage, thus attracting dues no higher than those levied on actually smaller vessels. And because of the influence of the beam measurement in the formula, it was also of interest to the shipowner to keep that figure as low as possible. The result was very deep, narrow ships, full-bowed and of almost square section for a good deal of their length. These characteristics caused such ships to be less stable than beamier vessels and slow in anything less than a gale of wind. It was said of the *William Miles* that she 'could never do more than eight knots, however hard it blew'. She was heavily built of pitch pine planking on oak frames and when she went ashore and capsized on Porthcawl Sands in August 1883 it is reported that she took a week to break up under the action of the sea, despite the fact that she was 67 years old.

Plate 11 (Below)

This photograph shows two typical deep-sea merchant sailing ships of the period before the development of the compound-engined steamship in the 1860s posed a serious threat. The vessel on the left is the *Mary Dugdale,* built at Kingston-upon-Hull in 1835 and shown lying in the River Tawe at Swansea in the mid-1840s. The deep, burdensome shape of her hull is very apparent, with little of the fine entry and run that we can see in later vessels. The decorative painted gunports along her side and the stern windows giving light to the master's and mate's accommodation aft are reminiscent of warships of the period. The *Mary Dugdale* was probably one of the Swansea copper ore fleet, bringing their cargoes across the Atlantic from the mines of Cuba or, sometimes, around Cape Horn after loading on the Chilean coast. Her upper yards have been sent down and her fore topgallantmast is housed on the foreside of the topmast—this was all part of the maintenance process of a wooden vessel with short-lived natural fibre rigging when in port.

Plate 12 (Below right)

This rare photograph shows the main deck of a merchant sailing vessel of the 1840s. She is undoubtedly ship- or barque-rigged and is contemporary with those in the previous photograph. She is probably lying at Swansea and may be the *Mary Dugdale* again. Unfortunately for us it seems that the lumpers are aboard and that cargo is being worked for the untidy jumble of ropes and gear on the fife rail and lying on the deck is not typical of the ship's

appearance when rigged for sea. Additionally, the crew, or maybe riggers from ashore, may well be undertaking maintenance work on the rigging, as in the contemporary photograph of the *Mary Dugdale,* and have caused temporary havoc whilst they renewed or turned end for end various of the halliards, braces and other running gear. Nevertheless, on to the fife rail at the base of the mainmast would be made fast the mainyard lifts, the function of which was to control each extremity of that particular yard and which could be used to cockbill the yard as has been done with the *Mary Dugdale.* The braces for all the yards on the mizzenmast (should the vessel be ship-rigged), the foot of which can be seen in the background of this photograph, would also be brought down to this rail. From here, then, each of the mizzen yards could be swung in order to trim the sails to the wind. (The main braces would be led aft to the mizzenmast and so down to a fife rail at the foot of that mast.) In addition to these elements of running rigging, the downhauls for the mizzen topmast and topgallantmast staysails would also be belayed on the main fife rail. These last two were to ensure that the fore-and-aft sails set on the stays which supported the mizzenmast could be brought in smartly when no longer needed. Each pin on this rail had its own rope, be it brace, halliard or downhaul, and this was not varied so that it was possible for each member of the crew to become accustomed to the arrangement and so place his hand on the required rope with no hesitation on the blackest night. However, as the saying goes, 'different ships, different long splices', and the arrangement could vary from ship to ship. The heavy purchase lying prominently on the deck may be in use for discharging cargo or, maybe, for helping in the execution of some heavy work aloft. Of interest here is the small hatchway in the left foreground, with two hatchboards removed, one of which is lying on its companions. Hatches in wooden sailing ships were kept as small as possible in order not to compromise the strength of the vessel's closely spaced deck beams and to afford as little opportunity as possible for a big sea breaking aboard to get below.

Plate 13 (Below)

Here, lying at Scarborough at the turn of the century, is the former Indian and Australian trader *Success,* built of teak at Moulmein in Burma in 1840. She is shown here on display to the public as a spurious former convict ship. Although at one time she seems to have been used as a reformatory ship, she did not transport convicts and is, basically, a merchant vessel in the tradition of those which traded to the Indian sub-continent under the aegis of the Honourable East India Company. Her rig, as seen here, is new but of immediate note is the depth and box-like construction of her hull. By the time the *Success* was built the tonnage law of 1773—which,

as was described in relation to the earlier photograph of the *William Miles* made a deep, narrow hull economically advantageous—was no longer in force, but shipowners and builders continued to be influenced by the customs and practices associated with the period before 1836 when the law was changed. It will be appreciated from this photograph that the *Success* bears all the characteristics of this tradition. Her entry and run are negligible, for the maximum width of the hull is carried far forward and aft, giving as great a cargo capacity as possible. Her hull is deep, (compare this photograph with Plate 19 of the *Berean* of 1869, a vessel of not so different

tonnage). Had the *Success* been built before the tonnage law was amended in 1836 this feature, and the length of her keel—almost the same dimension as the ship's length on deck—would have taken full advantage of its provisions; additionally increasing the vessel's capacity without prejudicing her calculated tonnage, for the formula specified by the tonnage law allowed for the keel length to be computed as the length on deck less three-fifths of the breadth. The *Success* was of 621 tons register which may be considered to be the optimum size of a big sailing merchantman in the 1840s. This tonnage would have allowed a deadweight (or cargo) capacity of 1,000 to 1,200 tons.

Plate 14 (Overleaf)

Unfortunately a frequent occurrence in the River Avon at Bristol, here is the ship *Importer* aground on a falling tide. The *Importer* was built in 1853 at New Brunswick, Canada, and was of 1,551 tons gross. The shipbuilding industry on the eastern seaboard of Canada was already firmly established when, in 1812, a duty was placed on the import of softwood into the United Kingdom from the Baltic. A resulting expansion of the Canadian timber trade gave a fillip to this relatively small scale industry and shipbuilding centres rapidly developed at New Brunswick, Nova Scotia, Prince Edward Island and Quebec. Timber for the construction of ships was plentiful and cheap in the great forests which came down to the water's edge and labour was easily available. At periodic times of depression the shipyard workers simply went back to employment on the farms and did not become a drain on a temporarily underemployed shipyard. But it was not often that these yards were silent, for Canadian

shipbuilding was able to make a uniquely significant contribution to the British shipping industry.

Normal practice elsewhere was to order ships when trade flourished but, as the inevitable trade cycle progressed, the vessels might not be delivered from the builders until trade had taken a down turn. Owners would then be left with ships for which few cargoes might be found until trade again improved. Canadian shipbuilders, however, made it possible for shipowners to take good, sound, new ships 'off the shelf' at a moment's notice and so take full advantage of times of prosperous trade, for from the early 19th century Canadians began building vessels not to order but on speculation and, thus, British shipowners were assured of a quick and ready supply of new tonnage in times of boom. When demand for ships was low, the builders themselves might put them into trade; often with timber outwards from Canada to the United Kingdom, carrying emigrants homewards. By the 1860s, however, the demand for wooden ships was falling as iron became cheaper and, in 1860, the duty on Baltic timber was removed. Wooden sailing ships nevertheless continued to be built in the Maritime Provinces of Canada until 1920. Compared with British-built vessels, those made in Canada tended to be much heavier looking with little or no sheer, a square midship section extending almost the entire length of the ship at deck level and a square, inelegant stern, much like American-built ships of this period. All of these features are apparent in the *Importer*. Her bows are less apple-cheeked than those of the ships in the previous photographs, with a much finer entry and, as can be seen from her circumstance here, she is not quite flat-bottomed. Of particular note are the ship's 'made' fore and main lower masts (that is, of composite construction and not from a single tree), bound with iron hoops. The heavy 'Armstrong's Patent' windlass, (the nickname arising because it was not connected to an engine but was operated solely by the muscle of the crew who might take more than two hours pumping at the long levers to bring in the anchor cable), can be seen on the forecastle head and is a typical item. Also typical is the white-painted deckhouse fitted into a hatchway from where it would have to be moved to gain access to the hold. A second equally small hatch is hidden by the ship's boats placed athwartships between the main and mizzen masts.

Plate 15

The same year that the *Importer* entered service the ship *Storm King* was launched from the Chelsea, Massachusetts, shipyard of John Taylor. The mid-1850s was the high point in the construction of American clipper ships and the *Storm King* was among the best known of these. After the discovery of gold in California in 1848 the classic trade of the American clipper was out from the East Coast of the USA around Cape Horn to San Francisco with passengers and cargo, then across the Pacific to load tea in China. On this occasion, however, the *Storm King* is shown lying in the Thames at Gravesend after her sale to British owners in 1863. Her upper topsail yards have been hoisted in the belief that to do so improved her appearance whilst in port. It seems likely that she would have once carried skysails above her royal yards. The *Storm King* was built to engage in those competitive and lucrative trades where speed was of the essence. Her cargoes, especially passengers and tea, were low density, high freight commodities and passage time between ports was required to be as short as possible. Passengers, understandably, were anxious not to lose any more working time than was necessary and, in the days before liner travel made a sea voyage a pleasure, wanted to be at their destination as quickly as possible. The same urgency applied in the tea trade, for the first cargoes home each year caught the best market. So, in those ships which we have come to regard as clippers, cargo capacity was sacrificed in the cause of fast passages. Comparison with the previous photograph of the *Importer* reveals this difference in emphasis. It can be seen that the *Storm King* has a very hollow bow and that her hull begins to narrow towards the stem from abeam of the foremast. The bows of the *Importer* seem, in comparison, to have been roughly shaped as late as possible, so preserving until the last moment the maximum capacity of her hold. The same can be said of the *Importer*'s stern, which maintains almost the same breadth as the vessel's midships section. Examination of the underwater lines of the *Storm King* would reveal much more shapely lines than those of the more box-like *Importer*, giving the former vessel a much smoother and faster passage through the water but restricting hold space considerably.

33

Plate 16 (Below)

When compared to the photograph of the *Storm King* of 1853, this vessel, the wooden ship *True Briton,* would appear to be of an earlier period. The large square ports beneath her quarterdeck and the projecting stern windows right aft are reminiscent of the ships of the 1840s described earlier. In fact the 'Blackwall Frigates', among which was numbered the *True Briton,* were direct descendants of the famous East Indiamen, operated so successfully by the Honourable East India Company. The *True Briton* was built in the Blackwall shipyard, from which many East Indiamen had been launched, in 1861 and traded under the house flag of Money Wigram, taking mostly first and second class passengers to Australia until 1880, making her one of the last of the great sailing passenger liners. Unlike the *Storm King,* built eight years earlier, the *True Briton* has the full bows and well rounded quarters characteristic of ships of the 1840s. Her standing rigging is powerful and her shrouds are brought down to chain plates far heavier than those of the *Storm King.* Like the clippers, however, the *True Briton*'s design reflects the nature of the trade in which she was engaged. Her passengers were people of the higher classes of society who paid for and expected a comfortable voyage to Australia free from avoidable alarms on passage and with as many creature comforts as were compatible with their shipboard environment. In contrast the clippers were engaged in a highly competitive arena, delivering to the goldfields of California (and later Australia) prospectors occupying dozens of cheap berths packed into the ships' holds. Fares were low and demand high so it was in the shipowner's interest to have fast ships which could make the extra voyage or so over a period. Although the Blackwall Frigates were often driven hard their voyages had little of the urgency of those of the clippers and were sedate in comparison. A fast clipper passage from the UK to Australia would have taken around 65 days whilst Blackwall Frigate times tended to be around two weeks longer. Under these circumstances there was little need for innovation in these ships and their traditional, conservative and ample lines persisted. Yet ships such as these were responsible for carrying many hundreds of emigrants to Australia. The *True Briton* is seen here lying at Gravesend on August 23 1871, the day that she sailed for Port Phillip, Southern Australia. The wooden erection between her fore and main masts is probably the housing for the cow which was carried on deck to provide fresh milk for the ship's passengers.

Plate 17 (Above)

Just three years after the *True Briton* was completed in 1861, this iron ship, the *Ranee,* formerly the *Cowasjee Jehangeer,* was built on the River Mersey. The transition from wood to iron in ship construction was not a smooth one on which a precise date can be placed. The revolutionary steamship *Great Britain* had been constructed with an iron hull as early as 1843, and ships incorporating wooden planking on an iron frame were built up to the mid-1870s. As we have seen, ships built of wood were still being launched in the 1860s. Once suitable iron had become cheap and plentiful enough to be used in shipbuilding its advantages over wood were soon apparent. As the volume of world trade increased in the mid-19th century, larger and larger ships were required. The dimensions to which wooden ships could be built were finite and iron (and later steel), due to its much greater strength, allowed

much bigger ships to be constructed. It was found that an iron ship was of considerably less weight than a wooden one of similar dimensions, for the plating of an iron ship is considerably thinner than the planking of a wooden vessel. This was in spite of the greater specific gravity of iron and the fact that, at first, much thicker plates and heavier frames were used than later experience proved to be necessary. In a wooden ship the hull and equipment accounted for about 40 per cent of the total displacement tonnage (that is, ship and cargo together), whereas in an iron ship the figure was about 30 per cent, allowing greater weight of cargo to be loaded aboard. Cargo capacity was further increased since the strength of iron allowed much smaller frames to be fitted than in a wooden ship, thus increasing space in a ship's hold. The frames of the *Ranee,* here seen under repair following a collision, can be seen to be of quite modest dimensions.

Plate 18 (Left) and Plates 19 and 20 (Overleaf)

These three photographs give us a good opportunity to study the underwater lines of three vessels, each of which have been described as clippers, and each built in 1869. Plate 18 is the Portuguese barquentine *Ferreira,* better known as the China tea clipper *Cutty Sark,* now restored and preserved at Greenwich. The very sharp entry and fine lines of this extreme clipper are clearly visible in this photograph, giving her an almost yacht-like appearance when compared with photographs of earlier vessels in this section. Although the *Cutty Sark* has achieved much fame and is undoubtedly a masterpiece of the naval architect's and shipbuilder's art, she can be considered to have been obsolescent for some three or four years at the time of her launch. On April 19 1866 the first of Alfred Holt's new compound-engined steamships, the *Agamemnon,* left London on her maiden voyage to China. She went out round the Cape of Good Hope, as did the clippers, and the economy of her engines and high pressure boiler was such that she consumed 20 tons or less of coal each day; equivalent to only 2¼lb of fuel per horse power per hour, a remarkable advance on the consumption of the old single-cylinder marine engines. On the return passage from China she carried some 2,800 tons of cargo and was less than 60 days on passage. In comparison the *Cutty Sark,* half the size of the *Agamemnon,* could carry only 600 tons of tea and was never less than 100 days on passage from China. She had difficulty finding tea cargoes from the very beginning and was 110 days from Shanghai on her maiden voyage. The *Agamemnon* was followed out to China by her sisters *Ajax* in June 1866 and *Achilles* in September.

A week before the *Cutty Sark* was launched the Suez Canal was opened. Of advantage only to the new steamships fitted with economical compound engines, this narrow waterway connecting the Mediterranean and Red Seas cut the passage from the UK to the Orient by some 3,000 miles, thus making further obsolescent the sailing vessel in that trade. So from the very first the *Cutty Sark* was in unequal competition with steamships which could now be operated economically on long routes, and she brought home her last cargo of tea from China in 1877, turning then to the Australian wool trade. The *Cutty Sark* is of composite construction, having

wooden planking over an iron frame, combining lightness with strength. Another reason for choosing to build the *Cutty Sark* this way was the belief that a wooden hull was preferable in the tea trade, for it was believed that an iron hull contaminated the cargo and caused condensation. More important than this, though, especially in a vessel trading to the tropics, was the consideration that a wooden hull could have satisfactory antifouling applied to it, in the form of copper sheathing, to restrict the accumulation of marine growth. Iron hulls had been sheathed but it was found that the close proximity of copper and iron set up galvanic action to the detriment of the hull. Whatever the reasons involved it must be said that the dozen composite ships built for the China trade in 1869 were the result of very conservative thinking on the part of their owners and not necessarily the result of an opinion that steamships could not compete on the route (for they were doing so successfully), but rather in the mistaken belief that the trade was sufficiently large to support both steamships and sailing vessels. There was also on the part of some traditionalist owners an unwillingness to abandon sail and an enthusiastic desire to produce ships which might be just that little bit faster than their rivals. It has been said that the *Cutty Sark* was built to beat the famous Aberdeen clipper *Thermopylae,* of 1868, and there may be much truth in this.

Also of composite construction was the barque *Berean,* Plate 19, built at Sunderland for the Australian trade. The *Berean* was of 542 tons gross as compared with the *Cutty Sark*'s tonnage of 963; the difference in length being 160 ft as against 212 ft. Despite this the *Berean* often gave good account of herself when sailing in company with larger vessels, including on one occasion the *Thermopylae.* She is seen here at Falmouth awaiting demolition not long after being sunk in collision on the Thames in 1910 (see Plate 96).

Plate 20 shows the American clipper *Glory of the Seas,* after use as a cold storage hulk, also awaiting her end in May 1923 when she was burnt for her metal. By far the largest of these three ships, she was of wooden construction and was of 2,009 tons gross and 240 ft long. Being entirely of wood, her framing was massive and took up far more room, proportionately, than did the frames of the composite vessels. The *Glory of the Seas* was the last sailing vessel built by the best known constructor of American clippers, Donald McKay at Boston, Massachusetts. Considered to be only a medium clipper, this ship lacks the fine hollow bow and round bilge of the *Cutty Sark* and is flat bottomed—the *Cutty Sark* could not sit on the mud like this! Nevertheless, in spite of her less refined lines, this vessel was fast, once reaching Newcastle, NSW, from San Francisco in 35 days.

The clippers have come to represent, in popular imagination, the epitome of the merchant sailing ship in the second half of the 19th century. It is a common belief that these ships, overburdened with canvas and with their decks constantly awash as they raced home from China, Australia or California, represent the typical square-rigger of the period.

Although the clippers can be considered to represent a stage in the development of the sailing merchantman, it must be pointed out that they comprised only a very small proportion of the fleets of the major maritime nations. That element of the British fleet that might be classed as 'clippers' can, perhaps, best be indicated by the following statistic. In 1870, the year which most concerns us here, the total net tonnage of sailing ships registered in British home ports was 4,578,000. In that same year 34 ships which might fairly be called clippers loaded the season's tea in Chinese ports for Britain. The total net tonnage of those 34 vessels was 28,726, representing a little more than half of one per cent of the total tonnage of British merchant sailing ships out of home ports. Even if all the other vessels

engaged in trades where speed was of importance are taken into account, the percentage of 'clippers' is unlikely to add up to much more than two per cent of the total.

Both gross and net tonnage have been mentioned so far and the distinction between the two measurements should now be explained. Neither is related to the weight of a ship or its cargo. Gross tonnage is an expression of the internal volume of a ship, less certain negligible areas, and 100 ft^3 of enclosed space is taken as one gross ton. Net tonnage is this figure minus non-earning space, such as crew accommodation. The latter figure therefore represents more truly than the former the actual space within the ship devoted to cargo. The term 'ton' in this instance derives from 'tun'—a large cask. The connection is readily apparent. The requirements of the majority of merchant sailing vessels were a balance of good cargo capacity, reasonable speed and low operating costs. The clippers, operating in high value trades where quick delivery was of the essence, with their big crews and small deadweight capacity, could only offer speed and, in the mainstream of trades, this was the least of the three considerations.

Plate 21

The iron ship *Cambrian Princess,* shown here anchored at Falmouth awaiting instructions regarding the port at which she was to discharge her cargo, can be said to be representative of the general cargo-carrying sailing ship of the latter part of the 19th century. Comparison with the photograph of the *William Miles,* built in 1816 (page 25), will show the extent of the development of the square-rigged ship under the stimulus of the competition of the compound-engined steamship during the period of great industrial expansion and the associated growth of world trade which followed the Industrial Revolution. The *William Miles* at 324 tons net, as built (she was lengthened in 1854), is not atypical of the large ocean trader of her time, whilst the tonnage of the *Cambrian Princess,* standing at 2,381 tons net is, similarly, the norm for the 1880s, representing a deadweight capacity of about 4,000 tons.

Paradoxically, however, the sailing vessel reached its most fully developed state at a time when that efficiency and economy of operation could no longer be fully exploited. After the middle of the 19th century the story of the development of the merchant ship is integral with that of the evolution of the iron and steel industries. Large ships could only be constructed of iron and steel, the size to which wooden ships could be built was finite; and larger and larger ships were needed if trade was to flourish. Iron and steel wire was required for the rigging of these big ships in order to take the extra stresses to which they were put. So as these materials became freely available and it became economically possible to build ships of them, more and more iron and steel sailing ships were launched. With new, stronger materials at his disposal the naval architect was able to redesign and refine the sailing ship. But, of course, these same advantages were also common to the steamship. Improved metals meant better propeller shafts, less liable to fracture, and stronger boilers able to withstand far greater steam pressure, so enhancing the efficiency and economy of the engine.

As merchant ships and barques reached their apogee in the latter part of the last century so also did the steamship. Three years before the completion of the *Cambrian Princess* in 1884, the Aberdeen Line steamship *Aberdeen* had sailed for Australia. She was fitted with the first triple-expansion marine steam engine to be used successfully on a long passage. This engine used the steam which was generated in the ship's boiler three times, instead of twice as with the compound engine. This resulted in yet further savings in fuel costs, eventually making the steamship a thoroughly practical proposition in all trades. Before it had reached its ultimate form, the sailing ship was being relegated more and more to the trades in low value, bulk commodities such as grain, ores, fertiliser and, notably, coal which was commonly taken abroad under sail to provide bunkers for the very steamships which were ensuring the decline in the world's fleet of sailing merchantmen.

The British home-registered fleet of sailing ships reached its peak of nearly five million tons net as early as 1865—it had already reached its maximum number of vessels two years previously. From that point onward a steady decline ensued until in 1883, the year that the ship in this photograph was laid down, the tonnage of steamships on the British register overtook that of sailing vessels, each totalling a little more than 3½ million tons. From thereon the decline of sail and the rise of steam was inexorable, although sail did for a short time increase its tonnage in the early 1890s. In 1897 Lloyd's underwriters increased sharply the insurance rates on sail tonnage, so accelerating the depletion of the fleets of British square-riggers. By the turn of the century there were seven million tons of steamships on the British register and only two million tons under sail.

The *Cambrian Princess,* built by Oswald Mordaunt of Southampton as the *Manydown,* passed to the Russian flag in 1914 then, following a dismasting, to the Italian flag. She ended her career as a hulk, a floating storage shed.

Plate 22 (Below)

The five-masted auxiliary barque *France* of 1912 does not strictly belong to this section devoted to the gradual evolution of the merchant sailing ship. She is rather an oddity but, nevertheless, her great size and powerful performance are due to the application of technology which had developed during the second half of the 19th century and which had given great impetus to the evolution of the square-rigger over that time. The *France* was the largest merchant sailing vessel ever built, measuring 5,633 gross tons on a length of 419 ft, and was launched at Bordeaux on November 9 1911, for the New Caledonia nickel ore trade to Europe. Her oil engines, driving twin screws, were of 295 Nominal Horse Power but, in common with all the large auxiliary sailing ships, were too feeble to make a significant contribution to the vessel's performance. Under sail alone the *France* was quite capable of making 14 knots, sometimes for days on end in favourable conditions, and in one 24-hour period averaged over 17 knots. Auxiliaries for ocean routes were a blind alley in the evolution of the commercial sailing ship. Their engines were generally underpowered and wasted space and crew. Those in the *France* were removed shortly before her loss in 1922. The *France* was fitted with many refinements normally only found in steamships, including electric lighting. Her crew, numbering around 50 men, were housed in the long bridge deck amidships. Even with so many men and extensive use of winches, the average time taken to

set all sail was about one and a half hours. In an interview in January 1922, whilst the vessel was lying in the Surrey Commercial Docks, London, after a voyage from New Zealand with a cargo of 11,000 bales of wool and 6,000 casks of tallow, the ship's Master told how the vessel had encountered a very bad hurricane whilst rounding Cape Horn. The high forecastle head, bridge deck and poop provided a relatively safe working area for the crew and only one sea had broken aboard, but unluckily this one wave not only did some damage but washed two of the *France*'s crew overboard. On her next homeward voyage, from New Caledonia with nickel ore, she drifted ashore on a coral reef soon after leaving port and was abandoned. Her hull was sold for a meagre £2,000.

Plate 23 (Overleaf)

The large four-masted barques of the 1880s and '90s can be said to represent that stage in the evolution of the ordinary square-rigged merchant sailing vessel at which greatest economy and efficiency was combined. Driven by the spur of competition and aided by new technology developed during the late 19th century, the deep-sea sailing merchantman had gradually reached a state of refinement which enabled a deadweight of 4,500 tons of cargo to be transported halfway round the world in about 100 days by a crew of little more than 20 men. The vessel in this photograph, the *Lawhill*, is typical of this last generation of square-rigged ships. She was built in 1892 by W.B. Thompson of Dundee and was of 2,942 tons gross. In spite of her large size Captain J.C.B. Jarvis had sailed this big barque whilst she was under the British flag with a crew of just 18 men. Unusually, as can be seen here, her topgallantmasts were fidded abaft the topmasts and not on the fore side as was the normal practice.

Ships such as the *Lawhill* have been described as huge floating warehouses and, indeed, to some extent, such they were. The low value bulk cargoes carried by these ships were not usually urgently required at the port of discharge as might be the case with consignments of machinery and other manufactured goods or, as we have seen, tea. Nor were such cargoes usually perishable. It was sometimes in the interest of the charterers for ships to be two or three months on passage for, in that time, a cargo might change hands several times with resultant profit to each speculator. Partly due to this, but more so to the economics of scale involved, there were in the late 19th century several trades in which steamship owners preferred not to engage but were content to leave to large sailing vessels. Whilst a steamship might take only half the time of a square-rigger to haul a cargo of nitrates from the west coast of South America, her running costs were far greater and this factor made her uneconomic in such trades, which involved long waiting in ports where cargoes were loaded very slowly from lighters or wagons. When one considers that the average merchant steamship of 1892 was of about the same tonnage as the *Lawhill* it can be more readily appreciated that a definite place for vessels under sail still existed at the end of the 19th century. In fact the last big square-rigged merchant ship to be built anywhere in the world, for the nitrate trade between Chile and Europe, the *Padua*, was not launched until 1926 (see Plate 116). Gustaf Erikson bought the *Lawhill* in 1917 and she was to become one of the mainstays of his fleet. She made a number of fast passages and more than earned her keep whilst under his flag, consistently earning good profits year after year. Between 1919 and 1941 her cargoes, both inward to Europe and outward, included wheat, timber, planed boards, saltpetre, guano and coal—all common cargoes for the last of the 'Tall Ships'.

Captain Erikson traded the *Lawhill* until 1941 when she was taken over by the South African government and condemned by a prize court. She was sold in 1946 and laid up. In 1950 she went aground and was broken up where she lay in 1957, just one year before the very last big steel square-rigged deep-sea merchant sailing ship in commission in the world sank in the South Eastern Pacific.

Plate 24 (Left)

This vessel is the four-masted iron ship *County of Kinross*, built in 1878 by Barclay, Curle and Company at Whiteinch on the River Clyde. She is somewhat smaller than the *Cambrian Princess*, shown in plate 21 (page 40), being of only 1,719 tons gross, but despite her extra mast, her sail area probably does not differ much from that of a three-masted ship. Relatively few four-masted ships were built, the four-masted barque being much the more popular rig. The *County of Kinross* is shown here at Barry in South Wales in the summer of 1897 undergoing repairs to her stem. On the night of June 18 1897, whilst she was lying at anchor in Barry Roads with a cargo of coal for Colombo, she was struck by the steamship *Coniscliffe*, outward bound from Barry to Marseilles. The collision smashed the *County of Kinross*'s bowsprit and caused heavy damage to her bows and fore rigging. Both ships put back into Barry for repairs and the *County of Kinross* was not able to resume her voyage until July 17.

Plate 25 (Right)

This photograph of the four-masted barque *Crown of Germany*, seen here in dry dock having her hull scraped and painted, shows very well the extremely full lines of the big carriers of the late 19th century. The *Crown of Germany* was built at Belfast in 1892 and was of 2,241 tons gross. Her depth of hold was more than 24 ft and her beam more than 40 ft. It can be seen that she is almost flat-bottomed and that her sides are quite vertical, giving her a very box-like appearance, thus enabling the greatest possible deadweight to be loaded within a hull length of 284 ft. Steam capstans were fitted to relieve the crew of the heaviest of work and patent halliard winches allowed four of the crew to hoist one of the heavy upper topsail yards in five minutes. The *Crown of Germany* was wrecked (as the German *Fischbek*) in the Le Maire Strait on August 6 1910 whilst bound for Cape Horn on a voyage from Port Talbot to Iquique.

The SEAMAN'S LIFE

Plate 26 (Right)

Members of the crew of the ship *Evesham Abbey,* 1,692 tons gross built in 1876, at Brooklyn in March 1894. They are, from the left: Harry Barron, the First Mate, aged 32; James Addison, the 30-year-old Second Mate; and David Thompson, an Able Seaman aged 23. Standing next to Thompson are two more Able Seamen: John Lucas, a 36-year-old Canadian from St Johns, Newfoundland, who deserted the ship a few days later so forfeiting his pay; and George Regan, 55 years old. Next to Regan is John Hammond, a 21-year-old Irishman who was probably a first-voyager since he was the only Ordinary Seaman aboard on this voyage. Completing the back row are John Dowler, AB, aged 27; William Carr, 22-year-old AB; and J.H. Brown, the coloured cook. Seated, from the left, is 'Scotty' (probably Henry Lovie, a 41-year-old AB from Aberdeen) with the ship's dog. Lovie signed the ship's articles with a simple cross, not being able to write his name. Next to him is the ship's carpenter, 55-year-old Isaac Jones, and on his left is Francis Rogers the sailmaker, aged 33. These last three are seated on the sailmaker's bench and Rogers occupies his usual working position. Beneath his legs is the canvas holdall which was fastened to the bench to take needles, grommets, etc, whilst close at hand are his fids, housed in holes at the end of the bench, which is edged to form a tray for small, loose items. If some of the older of these men seem even more elderly than their stated ages, it must be remembered that it was not uncommon for seamen, when signing on for a voyage, to knock a few years off their true ages to help convince the officers of their physical strength. Barron, the First Mate, signed on in 1893 for £8 per month, the Second Mate for £5 5s per month. The carpenter and sailmaker were paid £5 10s and £5 per month respectively, whilst the cook earned £4. The Able Seamen were each paid £2 15s per month and Hammond, the Ordinary Seaman, earned £2 10s. The Master's wages were a matter of negotiation between himself and the ship's owners, but may well have been £20 per month.

The *Evesham Abbey* was quite well manned, 19 Able Seamen and one Ordinary Seaman signing on in May 1893 in addition to the officers, petty officers, steward and cook; 27 in all. In 1926 the great four-masted barque *Herzogin Cecilie,* at 3,111 tons gross twice the size of the *Evesham Abbey,* rounded Cape Horn with a total crew of 19, but they were Ålanders bred to the sea and united by the ties of common loyalty to their community. Of the 19 ABs signed on the *Evesham Abbey* in Liverpool only seven signed off at Fleetwood in March 1895 after a voyage that had taken the ship to Calcutta, New York, Yokohama and Astoria on the west coast of the USA before sailing again for home. Of the remainder, the majority had been signed off at ports en route, had deserted or had been discharged through sickness. One was left behind in gaol at Calcutta having been given one month's servitude for wilful disobedience of a lawful command whilst on board.

Plate 27 (Overleaf top)

In 1906 the London shipowners Devitt and Moore bought the four-masted barque *Port Jackson* to be operated in the Australian trade as a cargo-carrying sail training ship. This scheme, developed in conjunction with the Marine Society, was intended to give square-rigged sea training to boys from the schoolship *Arethusa*. The *Port Jackson* was adapted to carry a maximum of 100 of these boys, between the ages of 14 and 18, and to give them training which would prepare them for entry into the Merchant Navy where the predominance of steamships was thought to preclude the possibility of a thorough training as a seaman. This photograph shows the *Port Jackson* moored at Gravesend, on the River Thames, on July 10 1885 under the ownership of Duthie Brothers and Company. She was built in 1882 by Alexander Hall and Company of Aberdeen and was of iron construction, having a gross tonnage of 2,212. To accommodate her boys, Devitt and Moore fitted the *Port Jackson* with a large deckhouse between the main and mizzen masts where the boat davits can be seen in this photograph. In her earlier days she had carried up to 480 emigrants in her 'tween decks.

Plate 28 (Overleaf bottom)

On September 2 1913 the *Port Jackson* sailed from Rotterdam bound for Australia with a full cargo of German coke and pig iron. In command was Captain Charles Maitland. Captain Maitland had joined the *Port Jackson* as Master in 1907 and remained with her until the ship was sold in 1916. In this photograph we can see him seated at the head of the saloon table in the company of his officers awaiting their luncheon at some time during that voyage. The officers of a deep-sea sailing ship lived and dined aft in accommodation which was usually situated under a short raised deck known as the poop, from which the ship was steered. The saloon was frequently decorated with rich panelling, as can be seen here, and lit by a skylight on the poop deck above. The cabins of the officers were arranged each side of the saloon. Of note here is the elegantly laid table, the steward at Captain Maitland's left shoulder and what appears to be the saloon piano at his back, under the clock. The First Mate, seen here third from the right, is W.H. Dowman. He had been in command himself under sail and was later to purchase at his own expense the famous clipper *Cutty Sark* from the Portuguese, thus ensuring her survival to this day.

Plate 29 (Above)

The ship's carpenter aboard the *Port Jackson* in 1913 was Mr A.G. Traill. This photograph was taken not aboard that ship but another owned by Devitt and Moore, and here Mr Traill poses in reflective mood by the capstan. He was a native of Peterhead and had spent three years in whalers out of that port at a time when 36 ships would leave to hunt whales each season. When he left Rotterdam in the *Port Jackson* in 1913, Mr Traill would have been very nearly 70 years of age. Captain Maitland himself was 64 years old, but the oldest hand aboard was undoubtedly the bosun who was 78! He had spent his entire career in sail and it was said that it was impossible to keep him out of the rigging. The advanced age of these men is indicative of the difficulty which was, at this time, experienced in signing on experienced hands to serve under sail, for the majority of seamen chose to serve in steamships where the work was less arduous, on deck at least, the pay was better, voyages were shorter and the risk

of accident or shipwreck less. A ship's carpenter, under sail, as well as being a seaman as able as any other aboard, also needed the skills of the blacksmith, block- and spar-maker, joiner, caulker and boatbuilder. In general, the maintenance of the structure of the ship, apart from the rigging and sails, was the carpenter's responsibility. This extended to sounding the wells to establish the depth of water in the bilges, keeping in good order the pumps which drew the bilge water out of the ship and, aloft, to keeping greased and in smooth working order all the gear which allowed the huge yards to swing efficiently and safely. Roughly dressed spare spars would be carried and, if needed through some calamity aloft, the carpenter would have been capable of preparing from them new yards or top- or topgallantmasts with only the resources available to him from his small workshop aboard. Any spare time that the carpenter might find would sometimes be filled by making furniture for the ship's Master.

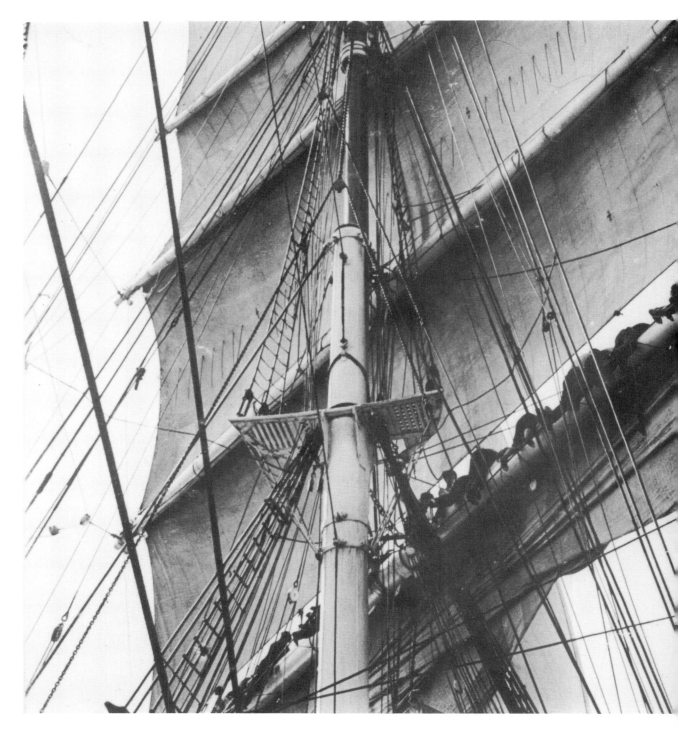

Plate 30

Here, the majority of hands aboard the *Port Jackson,* both cadets and sailors, are changing one of the big courses. Each of the lower sails on each mast was known as a course, and these were the largest sails set in a ship. In the case of the *Port Jackson* there were six square sails on each of three square-rigged masts in addition to the numerous fore-and-aft sails which included jibs, staysails and the spanker on the jigger mast. Each ship would carry two full suits of sails, plus spare sails and canvas to make good any damage or loss caused by heavy weather. Old, sometimes worn and patched sails, and sails of a light gauge of canvas, would be bent in fine weather latitudes—probably when entering the North East Trades on a south-bound voyage from the UK—in place of the new and heavy-gauge sails which would again be bent when the stormy latitudes below 40° South were entered. The task of changing every sail in the ship was an arduous and time-consuming one, often involving the off-duty watch as well as the watch on deck. The robands which attached the head of each of the square sails to the jackstay running along the top of its yard, would have to be cut away and the sail lowered with the buntlines and clewlines to the deck. There it would be rolled up, labelled and returned to the sail locker. Its replacement would be taken, tightly rolled again, from the locker and carried along the deck to the foot of its mast on the shoulders of the crew. Some of the biggest sails were very heavy indeed and often took the efforts of both watches to transport them. Once in place, stretched out along the deck under its appropriate yard, a gantline, or whip tackle, would be rigged on the mast, led to the capstan and used to hoist the sail up to the yard. The head earing cringles would be seized in place at the yardarms (as can be seen on the starboard yardarm in this photograph), and the crew would lay aloft to secure the head of the sail to the yard. This operation had to be repeated for every square sail in the ship.

Plate 31

Each Ordinary and Able Seaman in a deep sea sailing ship was required to become proficient at steering the vessel in every strength of wind from light airs to full gale. Here, judging by the rather aggressive stance of the officer on the left of the photograph, the hapless helmsman of the *Port Jackson* seems to have let the course wander a little. Behind him another of the ship's officers is taking a sight of the sun with his sextant and, no doubt, requires a steady platform on which to do so. Steering in a heavy, following sea, which could make the ship pitch and corkscrew, required both experience and stamina for the two-hour stretch which was each seaman's 'trick' at the wheel. Unlike the steamship sailor, if the helmsman of a square-rigger let his course swing he could bring the ship too far up into the wind, thus bringing the wind on to the wrong side of the sails and setting them aback. If this occurred in heavy weather a great deal of damage could result aloft and, if the ship broached-to, huge waves might come aboard and sweep anybody on the main deck over the side. In extremes of weather the helmsman would normally be given an assistant who would stand at the lee side of the wheel and help to restrain the violent kicks that it could give as the sea acted on the rudder below.

54

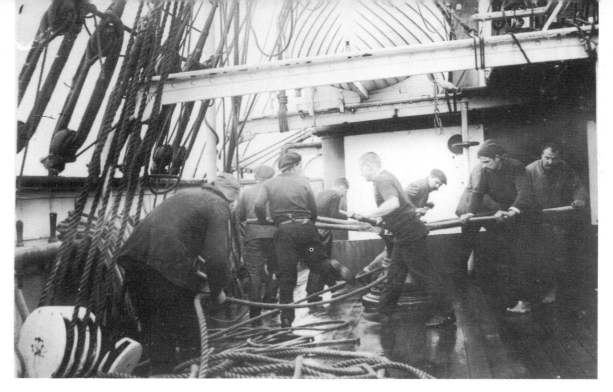

Plate 32 (Above)

Much of the really heavy work of 'pully-haul' aboard ship might be alleviated by taking a halliard, sheet or brace to one of the capstans fitted on the main deck in addition to a ship's main capstan on the forecastle head. In this photograph just such a capstan may be seen in operation aboard the *Port Jackson*. On this occasion it seems likely that the capstan is being used to hoist one of the heavy upper topsail, upper topgallant, or royal yards in order to set the sail. The *Port Jackson* had nine such yards. To set the sails on these yards a man would first be sent aloft to cast off the gaskets used to hold the sail furled to its yard. Then the yard would be hoisted up its mast, the sail sheeted home and the buntlines overhauled by the seaman who went aloft to cast off gaskets. This was done to prevent chafe on the belly of the sail. On taking in the sail the yard halliard would be let go in which case, in good weather conditions, the yard might come down its mast under its own weight. Downhauls were fitted should it prove necessary to give the yard some help. The sail could then be bunted up and furled along the yard in the usual manner. The capstan could also be used to 'freshen the nip' (or sweat-up) on any sheet, tack or brace which had slackened under prolonged tension.

Plate 33 (Right)

A common, if alarming, pastime aboard merchant sailing ships was fishing for sharks. Here is one brought aboard the *Port Jackson* on June 2 1914 in a position 3°N 26°W in the area of calms known as The Doldrums. The usual bait was a chunk of salt pork from the ship's rations attached to a strong steel hook. In the photograph the bait may be seen still on the hook. The bait and hook was trailed astern over the poop rail on a stout line with, perhaps, a chain trace between hook and line. Once a shark took the bait all available hands would rush to haul the unfortunate creature inboard, often with the assistance of a bowline around its tail. Once aboard the shark was usually quickly despatched and often its stomach was opened to reveal whether or not an unlucky sailor had formed part of its recent diet. In the case of this particular beast the stomach was found to be empty. A common superstition held that a breeze would spring up following the killing of a shark, making the capture of one in The Doldrums especially welcome. The shark's jaw with its row of savage teeth would be removed and preserved as a memento, its backbone could be fashioned into a walking stick and its tail used to decorate the end of the jibboom and so ensure fair winds.

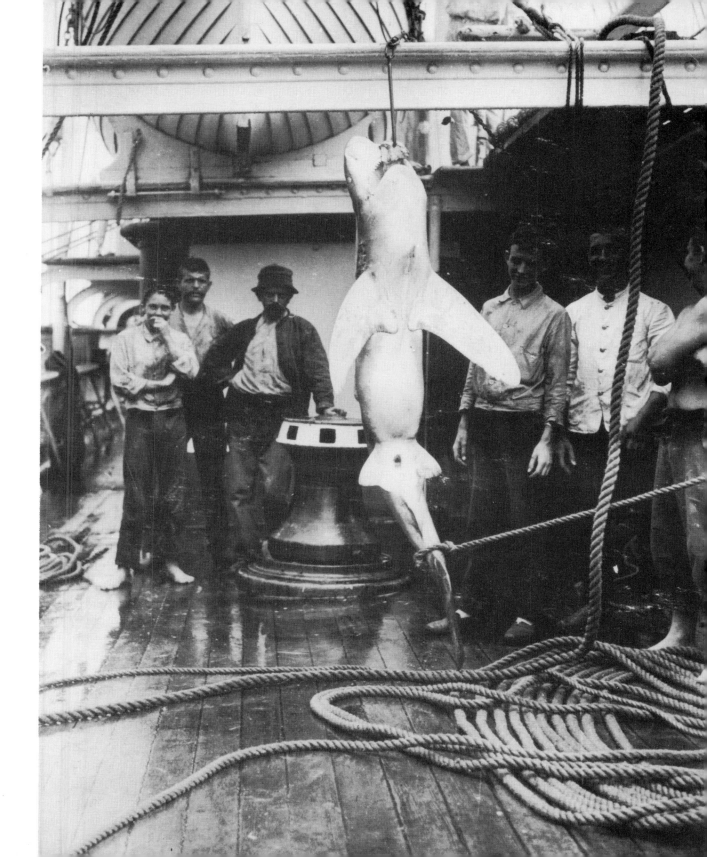

Plate 34 (Below)

The large expanses of wooden decking, common even in iron- and steel-hulled sailing vessels, were kept clean and white by laboriously rubbing them over with sandstone and water. This task, known as 'holystoning', was performed with blocks of sandstone known as 'bibles', or 'prayerbooks' for smaller areas. The practice of kneeling to the task no doubt gave rise to the terms! Here some of the *Port Jackson*'s cadets rub down the poop deck under the watchful eye of one of the petty officers. In earlier times it was not uncommon for shipmasters and mates to allocate Sunday, usually a rest day, to this task, giving rise to the 'Philadelphia Catechism', familiar among seamen: 'Six days shalt thou labour and do all that thou art able, and on the seventh holystone the deck and scrape the cable!'.

Plate 35 (Right)

In spite of the undisputed hardships and privations endured by the sailing ship seaman, life in a big square-rigger could very often be both exhilarating and exciting. This is not to detract from the fact that it was more frequently wet, cold, wearying or hungry. The thrilling spectacle of a big ship or barque heeling under full sail with all her canvas drawing to a strong breeze; pitching maybe into a head sea and throwing spray, and sometimes green water, back over her forecastle head, whilst the wind roared in her rigging, was a sight which has caused many of the chroniclers of deep-sea sail to aspire to heights of evocative and lyrical prose. Perhaps the best situation from which to witness the grandeur of a ship under sail was the bowsprit. In this photograph one of the *Port Jackson*'s cadets leans back against the bowsprit guy, watching the big barque as she sails close-hauled on the starboard tack making, perhaps, some eight or nine knots.

Plate 36 (Above)

The steel barque *Garthsnaid*, of some 1,400 tons gross, was completed by A. McMillan and Son Ltd, of Dumbarton, in June 1892 as the *Inversnaid* for George Milne and Co of Aberdeen. During the First World War she was sold to Sir William Garthwaite, Bart, and a little later her name was changed to *Garthsnaid* to comply with the style of nomenclature of the rest of the Garthwaite fleet. It is under this name that she is seen here anchored at Falmouth awaiting notification of the port at which she is to discharge her cargo. Sir William was one of the very last shipowners to trade square-riggers under the British flag and, although his office was in Paris, his fleet of sailing vessels was operated by a subsidiary company, the Marine Navigation Company of Canada Ltd, some vessels being registered in the UK and some, like the *Garthsnaid*, at Montreal.

Early in 1923 the *Garthsnaid* sustained severe heavy weather damage whilst on a voyage from Iquique and was towed into Melbourne, 101 days out, by the White Star liner *Zealandic* on April 3. She had lost her mainmast, her fore and mizzen topmasts were damaged and her windlass smashed. The bill to her owners for the tow was £15,000 and damage to the ship amounted to £8,000. In 1916 she had cost Garthwaite £13,000 to buy and so, in the circumstances, was not worthy of repair, ending her career as a hulk at Melbourne.

This photograph, and the succeeding pictures of the *Garthsnaid*, were very probably taken by the barque's Second Mate, Mr Turner, whilst on a voyage from Iquique to Delagoa Bay in 1919. It is due to his tenacity with a camera—not an easy task on the wet, pitching deck of a sailing ship—that some of the finest photographs of life aboard a deep-sea square-rigged ship have been made and preserved.

Plate 37 (Right)

Here a large wave breaks aboard the *Garthsnaid*, probably whilst on a voyage from Iquique to Delagoa Bay soon after the First World War. A heavy sea such as this could fill the main deck and often the water had not drained from the deck before the next wave broke aboard. In spite of this the crew would still have to attend to the running rigging as required, pulling on braces, buntlines and clewlines as seawater swirled about their legs and great seas poured aboard. The galley was usually situated on the main deck and many a kid of hot food has been washed into the scuppers on its way forward to the forecastle where the crew lived and messed. In this photograph it can be seen that a lifeline has been rigged along the length of the deck to help the crew move about more safely.

Plate 38 (Left)

The view from the port main yardarm of the *Garthsnaid,* at sea in a moderate swell soon after the First World War. Right aft, on the poop deck, can be seen the helmsman at the wheel. The fact that he is apparently alone in conning the ship might be accounted for if it was the Second Mate, Mr Turner, who was the officer of the watch and had left his post on the poop to take this photograph. Forward of the wheel can be seen the saloon skylight and scuttle giving access to the officers' accommodation. The helmsman steers by a small compass mounted on the skylight but the ship's main binnacle may be seen between the boats on the bridge forward of the mizzenmast.

Plate 39 (Right)

Moving about the slippery deck of a sailing ship hard on the wind in heavy weather could be very hazardous. In this photograph, the *Garthsnaid,* braced up hard on the starboard tack, gives a roll to port. Lifelines have been rigged and some of the running rigging taken up on to the bridge alongside the boat in order to make the seamen's work less dangerous. The *Garthsnaid* seems to be shortened down to just lower topsails and staysails; all she might carry in a strong gale.

Plate 40 (Above)

The sailing ship seaman needed, among his many
other talents, quite a considerable amount of the skill
of a steeplejack. Confidence and agility aloft were
essential attributes if a seaman was to operate
efficiently in all extremes of weather, often in total
darkness, at heights of up to 200 ft above the deck.
In all but the best weather conditions the old maxim
'One hand for the ship and one for yourself' was
often impossible to apply and might have brought a
hollow laugh from a sailor accustomed to wrestling
with a sodden, icy topsail, 90 ft above a pitching deck
in a stormy gale. This photograph, however, shows a
scene aboard the *Garthsnaid* in a flat calm. Six
members of the watch are bending a new main
topgallantsail. Sails were changed regularly in this
fashion throughout a long voyage; older, weaker sails
for fine weather latitudes being replaced with new,
strong canvas for latitudes where bad weather might
be expected.

Plate 41 (Below)

The first step in taking in a sail was to clew and bunt it up to the yard. This was done from the deck and drew the sail up under the yard somewhat in the fashion of a venetian blind. The buntlines led from the foot of the sail directly up to the yard, across to the mast and down to the deck. Here two buntlines can be seen on the lower topsail of the *Garthsnaid,* leading up through their circular thimbles over the belly of the sail. Clew lines led from the lower corner, or clew, of the sail again up to the yard and down to the deck. By hauling on all these lines the sail could be brought up to the yard. It was then for the crew to go aloft and out on to the yard in order to furl the sail, which was manhandled and rolled tightly until it lay snug along the top of the yard. Here the watch on the *Garthsnaid* have achieved this on the mainyard and are passing lines known as gaskets around the yard and sail to keep the latter firmly in place.

Plate 42 (Left)

The *Garthsnaid,* homeward bound in the North East Trades. All square sail is set and drawing nicely to a fine breeze on the starboard tack. Good weather such as this gave a ship's crew a chance to make good some of the wear and damage which had occurred to her gear and rigging during the long periods of heavy weather in Southern latitudes. Here two seamen can be seen on the top of the fore lower mast repairing or replacing some of the running rigging on the foresail. There were no idle moments aboard a square-rigger; there was always some part of the miles of wire, chain and rope which required attention and overhauling.

Plate 43 (Right)

The four-masted barque *Medway* was another of Devitt and Moore's commercial training ships but, unlike the *Port Jackson,* was built with sail training and not profit uppermost in mind. When Devitt and Moore bought her in 1910 she was already fitted with a large lecture area under the poop and spacious deckhouses to accommodate her cadets. A. McMillan and Son of Dumbarton had built her in 1902 for Spanish owners, although they registered her at Montevideo, under the Uruguayan flag. Until Devitt's renamed her in 1910 she had carried the name *Ama Begonakoa.* Unusually, she was fitted with two deep-tanks each capable of holding 750 tons of water ballast each. Although a double success as a cargo-carrier and a training ship, the unusual conditions prevalent during the First World War forced Devitt and Moore to sell the *Medway.* In 1918 she was taken to Hong Kong where she was unrigged and converted to a diesel-powered tanker for the Anglo-Saxon Petroleum Co Ltd; a suprising end to the last of Devitt's big square-riggers.

Plate 44 (Above)

Raising anchor on those ships without a steam donkey boiler which could be connected to the windlass was a task involving most of the crew. When anchoring, a ship might run out as much as five shackles, some 450 ft of chain cable, to gain a firm hold on the ground. All of this heavy cable had to be brought back by the capstan in the case of the *Medway.* Here we see the crew of that barque at the capstan bars bringing the ship up to the anchor. Once the cable had been hove short sail would be loosed and, as the anchor cable lay no more on the sea bed but was 'up and down', or led straight from the anchor itself to the hawse, the order 'break her out' would be given and the ship would be free. Using the capstan, it often took hours to weigh anchor. Sitting atop of the capstan can be seen the shantyman with his fiddle. Shanties were sung at the capstan to co-ordinate the efforts of the men at the capstan bars. One or two 'shirkers' can be seen in this photograph!

Plate 45 (Below)

Boat drill aboard the *Medway* during a voyage from New York to Adelaide in 1912. Some impression of the difficulty involved in putting a heavy ship's boat in the water using these old-pattern radial davits can be gained from this photograph. It could be a time-consuming operation, dangerous if the ship was going down. It became even more inconvenient if launching on the weather side when the wind would hold the boat inboard, or if the ship was listing, often making it impossible to launch boats on the higher side of the ship. Frequently, in heavy weather, shipmasters would make no effort to lower a boat in an attempt to rescue a man fallen overboard. The time involved in heaving-to a big square-rigger and lowering a boat often made an attempt at rescue impracticable. In the 19th century sailing ships often carried their boats capsized and lashed down on the deckhouses and, frequently, they were used as repositories for livestock or coals. In this photograph, however, the weather is calm and the operation not so very arduous. The lady spectator, standing beneath the awning rigged to provide shade, may be a passenger or the wife of one of the ship's officers (see Plate 48).

Plate 46

Wet work aboard the *Medway* in 1912. A big four-master under sail in these conditions could often make 14 knots but it was wearying to the crew who would frequently be soaked in spite of their oilskins and exhausted with the continual hard labour required to work the ship in extremes of weather. In this photograph several of the seamen seem to be having difficulty in keeping their feet on the rolling deck, made more hazardous by waves of dead water rushing across it.

Plate 47

Unlike the unfortunate crew of the *Port Jackson,* shown in Plate 34, these four seamen from the *Medway*'s crew have long-handled scrubbers to take their 'holystones'. The slurry left behind by the gradual erosion of the sandstone on the deck can be seen in this photograph but would soon have been washed over the side by a few buckets of seawater or by a hose connected to the ship's saltwater pump. Lying along inside the bulwarks, below the rail, is a very large baulk of timber which might easily be fashioned into a replacement topgallant mast should damage aloft make it necessary. Uppermasts and yards were often replaced by the crews of ships at sea after heavy weather had caused partial dismasting. The craft of the rigger was all part of the sailor's art.

73

Plate 48 (Left)

Devitt and Moore's barque *Medway* was a training ship as well as earning her living by carrying cargo. Here is Captain Noakes, the *Medway*'s nautical instructor, on the poop deck with his wife and two children. Captain Noakes, who had been Principal at a nautical school in London, was aboard to teach the ship's cadets the intricacies of navigation and seamanship. He had spent some time in sailing ships himself, including a period as Second Officer of the famous Aberdeen clipper *Thermopylae*. Although today it is commonplace for ship's officers to be accompanied on voyages by their wives (if not their families), in the deep-sea sailing vessel it was usually only the Master who had that privilege. Many shipmasters' wives became adepts at navigation and ship handling and many a Master's children were perfectly at home in the hair-raising playground of a ship's rigging. Notice the rather urbane look of the helmsman, obviously giving an old shore-going suit its last lease of life.

Plate 49 (Above)

Among the routine tasks of maintenance to be performed aboard a square-rigger, that of overhauling the scores of blocks that kept the running rigging operating efficiently, was among the most important. If the gear of a sailing ship was to respond quickly and the crew was not to be exhausted by heaving on reluctant braces and halliards, then the blocks (or, perhaps to the landsman, 'pulleys'), through which the rope, wire and chain ran needed to be free. Every so often each of these blocks was sent to the deck for maintenance and lubrication. The pin was withdrawn from the shell, or outer casing, thus releasing the sheave. In this photograph, which shows members of the *Medway*'s crew at this task, the kneeling figure is shown at work on a treble block. His left hand is on the shell and at his feet can be seen two sheaves and a pin. This was often a dirty job since black lead was used as a lubricant.

Plate 50 (Above)

A regular companion of ships at sea in southern latitudes, the albatross is perhaps the most romantic of seabirds. Achieving a wing span of up to 15 ft, the albatross is capable of great endurance at sea and the same birds have been observed to follow ships for many days at a time. Whilst being supremely graceful and accomplished in flight, the albatross is clumsy on the ground and after landing, or being enticed onto a ship's deck, would find great difficulty in getting airborne again. In this photograph four of these splendid seabirds get rough treatment from the crew of the *Medway*. Their beaks are held shut, for the albatross can inflict a painful bite with its long, hooked beak. In this case, however, it seems no lasting harm will come to the birds for the crew have put collars giving the ship's name and position, together with the date, around their necks, no doubt with the intention of releasing them to be encountered by other ships in the future (Plate 77).

Plate 51 (Right)

Three of the *Medway*'s crew work out on the bowsprit, handing the jibs. This is a calm day and there is little danger to the seamen but in heavy weather the bowsprit was one of the most hazardous places to be aboard ship. In anything of a sea, a sailing ship would pitch appreciably and, in the roughest of weather, might throw green water over her forecastle head. Then anyone working on this spar would really have to hang on to avoid being swept off. A few vessels, training ships particularly, carried a netting arranged under the bowsprit to prevent anyone falling from it dropping into the sea, where the unfortunate sailor might be swept straight under the ship's hull. In common with the large majority of merchant sailing vessels, however, the *Medway* carried no such netting. In the fine weather shown here this was a pity, for it was a splendid place to lie in calm sunny conditions out of the Mate's eye!

76

Plate 52

The four-masted barque *Passat* of 1911 had the
distinction of flying the house flag of perhaps the two
most famous owners of deep-sea sailing ships in the
20th century. She was built in Germany by Blohm
and Voss at Hamburg for the Laeisz concern, the
famous 'Flying P' line who were to place an order for
a four-masted barque to be built as late as 1926. The
Passat was built for the trade to the west coast of
South America where she loaded nitrates for use as
fertiliser and in the manufacture of explosives in
Europe. In 1932 she was acquired by the equally
well known Finnish shipowner Gustaf Erikson and
she joined his famous 'grain fleet' of sailing ships
registered in the Åland islands at the mouth of the
Gulf of Bothnia. The *Passat* is seen here towing up
Channel in September 1933, inward-bound from
Wallaroo, South Australia, with a cargo of grain.
The *Passat* is still afloat, much changed from her
days as a merchant ship, as a stationary museum and
schoolship at Travemünde in Germany.

Plate 53 (Below)

The *Passat*'s last voyage under Erikson's flag began at Port Talbot in December 1948. Gustaf Erikson had died in August 1947, aged 75, and his son Edgar was in control of the company. Together with the *Pamir,* the *Passat* loaded one of the last two cargoes of grain to be brought from Australia in a square-rigger. Aboard her on that outward trip was a lady passenger and a stewardess, Miss Anne Stanley, who took a large number of fine photographs of life aboard, from which this small selection is made. The *Passat* left Port Talbot early in the morning of December 18 1948 with a total of 34 crew under Captain Ivar Hägerstrand, one of the most experienced surviving sailing ship Masters. Later that day the officers picked the watches and this photograph shows the selection under way. Normally the whole crew joined together to get a ship to sea and only when she was on passage, under sail, would the crew be divided into watches. The *Passat* worked a two-watch system giving the crew four hours on duty and four hours off. As can be seen in this photograph, although the ship is at sea she is not yet 'shipshape' and there is a lot of loose gear lying about.

Plate 54 (Right)

On January 10 1949 the *Passat* was in Latitude 1°20′N Longitude 22°8′W, a little north of the Equator and in the area between the Northeast and Southeast trade winds known as The Doldrums. Here a ship could be kept for weeks in seemingly endless calms, gradually inching her way forward by trimming the sails to every chance breeze—heavy work for the crew continually swinging the ponderous yards. In times of flat calm, however, there were always other tasks to be allocated to the crew and one of the favourites with shipmasters was the detested task of chipping rust. This photograph shows one of the *Passat*'s crew chipping rust and painting the hull with red lead. On this occasion the ship was making way through the water and the Master was a little worried, for whereas a fall from aloft is accidental, a man falling from a stage over the side and being eaten by sharks is the skipper's responsibility since, strictly, no man is allowed over the side at sea.

Plate 55 (Left)

The seaman's life aboard a square-rigger at sea consisted not only of routine adjustments to the sails and yards as weather conditions dictated but was a continual routine of repair, replacement and overhaul of the ship's complex gear. Here the Second Mate and three of the *Passat*'s crew are setting up a new forestay. This stay, of heavy wire cable, is anchored at the forward end of the forecastle head, where these men are standing, passes up and around the head of the fore lower mast and back to the forecastle head. Each lower mast in a sailing ship has its own stay, leading forward, as does each topmast and topgallantmast. These stays support the masts against pressures tending to topple them backwards whilst the shrouds, leading down to each side of the ship, prevent the masts toppling forwards or sideways under pressure. All these stays and shrouds are part of the ship's standing rigging.

Plate 56 (Above)

January 11 1949, just a few miles north of the Equator. Here the steward of the *Passat,* Axel Lundgren, is washing soiled cabin linen in a tub on deck. The steward was one of the 'idlers' aboard a sailing ship, not standing a watch and not, under normal circumstances, assisting in the sailing of the ship. He was usually accommodated aft and his duties were confined to attending to the needs of the officers and passengers, if any. The crew fetched their own food from the galley, taking turns to be messman. Despite his less energetic duties, Axel Lundgren has been described by one of the crew on that trip as 'the strongest man I have ever known'.

Plate 57 (Left)

Furling the mizzen royal on February 22 1949 at the beginning of the long crossing of the Indian Ocean to Australia. The day had begun fine with a good breeze driving the *Passat* before it and giving her a heel of some 12°. As the day wore on, however, the barometer began to drop and the Master, Captain Hägerstrand, decided to reduce sail. The starboard watch was sent aloft to take in the royals and at four o'clock the wind veered until it was right aft and heavy rain began to fall. The heavy list to starboard, apparent in this photograph, means that the men on the royal yard, 150 ft above the waterline, would have the sea vertically below them and not the ship's deck.

Plate 58 (Right)

A candid photograph of the *Passat*'s First Mate on the deck at the foot of the mainmast. This was one of the last two deep-sea voyages by European merchant sailing ships ever made and at this very late stage it was proving exceptionally difficult to find crews. Gustaf Erikson, owner of the *Passat,* and his son Edgar, who succeeded him and who is Chairman of the highly successful Rederei Gustaf Erikson today, recruited their Masters and Mates exclusively from the Åland Islands, the only major town of which is Mariehamn, home port of the *Passat.* But in 1949 the supply of officers capable of running a big square-rigged ship was diminishing rapidly. The officers in later Erikson ships tended to be men dedicated to sail. These last two voyages, by the *Pamir* and *Passat,* were in the way of being a post-war experiment by Edgar Erikson for, if the supply of officers was thin, the number of qualified seamen willing to ship aboard his vessels was more so. Until Alan Villiers shipped aboard the *Lawhill* in 1921, Erikson had normally employed only Ålanders in his forecastles and continued to recruit as many as he was able thereafter. He was aided by the requirement for every aspiring officer in the Finnish merchant navy to have experience under sail. Here was a ready supply of young crews. There was also a number of Germans eager for berths to enable them to meet sail training requirements. Latterly, however, these requirements were abolished, the dwindling number of sailing vessels making them impractical.

The age of what might be called the 'romance of the sailing ship' perhaps began in the 1920s, encouraged by the writings of enthusiasts, Villiers among them. An increasing number of adventurers, from all over Europe, Australia and the USA, began to seek berths aboard the last 'Tall Ships'. Most of them were young and few were seamen by profession. Apprentices paid a premium of £50 for the privilege of sailing in one of Erikson's square-riggers. The fact that such youthful inexperienced crews, among whom might be only a few Ålanders with the necessary practical skills to train the remainder, were able to sail the big four-masters between Europe and Australia, is indicative of their dedicated zeal and the high quality of the officers who led them. In spite of the paring of expenses, the post-war voyages were financially unsuccessful and, on arrival in Penarth the *Pamir* and *Passat* were laid up and used as floating grain warehouses. Both were later bought for sail training ships, the *Pamir* being lost in 1957.

The absence of elaborate ceremony on these later ships whilst in trade can be gauged from the unarchetypal appearance of this officer's uniform. Although he wears a uniform jacket, his trousers are essentially working dungarees and his cap is, no doubt, more comfortable than a stiff uniform cap. On his shoulder is Eustace, one of the ship's cats.

Plate 59 (Below)

A fine view of the forecastle head of the *Passat* showing her rigged for sea. In the centre of the photograph is the capstan which, among other tasks, could be used to weigh anchor, the chain passing around the windlass on the deck below which is operated directly via the capstan. The long white bar pivoted just forward of the capstan is the anchor crane, used to bring the anchors aboard when the ship was clear of land and to hoist them outboard in readiness for dropping. The anchors themselves can be seen bolted down to the deck on either side of the forecastle head in the position they occupied when the vessel was at sea. (One has the fog horn lashed to it.) Shortly before they were required they would be lifted outboard by the crane and secured with a chain lashing. By this time the anchor cables would have been shackled to the anchors. A tripping mechanism (which can be seen beneath the shanks of the anchors in this photograph) would be employed to release the chain lashing when the anchors were let go.

Plate 60 (Right)

This photograph was taken on March 10 1949 when the *Passat* was less than three weeks away from Australia. The ship made a good speed in heavy weather during this day, running at between 10 and 14 knots and rolling from between 5° to starboard to 30° to port. Anne Stanley describes the thrill of being on deck in such weather and says that some of the seas were 'higher than houses'. This photograph shows the *Passat*'s main steering position, amidships on the bridge deck. In really heavy weather four seamen may have had to man this double wheel to keep the ship on course. On this occasion two men were required. The windward helmsman wears a safety harness to prevent him being thrown right over the wheel should it give a strong kick; an accident which resulted in injury to many a seaman. By his right foot is the brake to restrain the wheel should he lose control.

Plate 61 (Below)

On March 30 1949 the crew of the *Passat* received their first mail for 103 days and some of the anticipation and merriment which this engendered can be seen in this photograph. There is no doubt that the closed, almost monastic, life of the crew of a ship at sea for months at a time (entirely isolated from the rest of humanity in the case of those vessels, which carried no radio), contributed much to the sailing ship seaman's unique character. Self-reliance, tenacity and perseverance and—in many cases despite the more often than not true stories of rip-roaring indulgences in port—a taciturn reservedness, were common traits of the 19th (and 20th) century shellback. There has been no other activity on earth, save that of the more rigorous monastic orders, which has enforced such a prolonged removal of an individual from society than that of seafaring under sail.

Plate 62 (Below)

At 11.30 am on Tuesday, March 29 1949, the *Passat* dropped anchor over the ballast grounds five miles from Port Victoria, Southern Australia. One mile astern lay her sister ship, the *Pamir*. In this photograph more of the crew than are probably necessary are lifting the gangway davit into position. Being no exception to the rule, the crew's enthusiasm to get the ladder rigged and to get ashore after more than 100 days at sea can be judged from their application to this task! For the next few days life aboard the *Passat* was more than a little lively.

Plate 63 (Left) and Plate 64 (Overleaf)

These two photographs show the iron ship *Dunbritton*, built at Dumbarton in 1875, loading, and under sail with, a cargo of sawn timber early in 1903. Plate 63 shows the ship at Port Blakely, in Puget Sound on the Pacific coast of the United States. Puget Sound, adjacent to the extensive fir forests of the American northwest, was an important area for the export of lumber and sawn timber, including spruce, cedar and pine. An elaborate system of ramps has been rigged up to and across the *Dunbritton*'s poop, along which the timber could be drawn until it reached the main deck from where it could be passed to the hold. In contrast, the vessel alongside—the Norwegian wooden barque *Excelsior* of 1891—is bows-on to the quayside and has a port low down in her bows through which lengths of timber could be passed direct to the hold. Once loading had finished a square section of planking could be replaced in the port and would be securely caulked and held in position with a strongback (fitted inside the hold), to ensure a close, tight fit. This could not be done in an iron ship like the *Dunbritton* and, in her case, the lumber or timber had to be passed down into the hold through the small hatchways on the main deck.

Plate 64 shows the *Dunbritton* at sea on her way from Port Blakely to Fremantle, in Australia, where she arrived in June 1903 after a passage of four months. It can be seen that she carries a deck cargo of timber in addition to that in her hold. As timber is relatively light, this could be done without loading the vessel down below her marks. The disadvantage was that it made the crew's work additionally uncomfortable and hazardous. Any sea breaking aboard might sweep an unwary seaman over the side for he no longer had the protection of high bulwarks to prevent him. Work on deck, in the dark, would become more difficult with the uneven surface of the deck cargo under the crew's feet. In this photograph it can be seen that some of the running gear has been coiled down on top of the cargo to make access easier.

91

Plate 65 (Above)

Discharging a cargo of coal from the hold of the barque *Invercauld* anchored at one of the nitrate ports on the west coast of South America. Unlike steamships, with their sophisticated cargo-handling gear, sailing ships were not fitted with derricks and the ship's rigging made quayside discharge of bulk cargoes by grab difficult. Instead a tackle would be rigged to the lower yard over each hatchway and tailed down, sometimes to a steam winch if the ship was so fitted or, as in this case, to a portable dolly winch. This was work for the whole ship's crew and the labour involved in discharging maybe 3,000 tons of coal in the stifling heat of the South American climate can be imagined. The baskets seen here being emptied into the lighter alongside were filled by members of the crew working with shovels in the hold. It was usual for the charter party of a sailing ship to stipulate that a rate of discharge of 100 tons of cargo per working day be achieved. Numerous delays, frequently caused by sea conditions in the exposed anchorages of the west coast ports, kept the majority of sailing ships at anchor for as much as three months, discharging and taking in ballast and cargo.

Plate 66 (Left)

Water ballast, taken aboard a ship to keep her stable at sea when empty of cargo and carried in specially designed compartments, usually constituting wing tanks or a double bottom, was introduced in the 1850s. It was, however, little used aboard sailing vessels. Instead a 'stiffening' of gravel or stones was put into the bottom of the hold. Without this ballast the tall, weighty masts and yards of an empty sailing ship would make the ship exceptionally 'tender' and might easily turn her over. The *Moshulu,* a four-masted barque of roughly the same tonnage as the *Passat,* took some 1,500 tons of ballast to make her safe; the *Passat*'s cargo capacity was some 4,500 tons. Once in the ship the ballast had to be confined on the floor of the hold between shifting boards and with a false floor of heavy boards built over it, for if once it began to move as the ship rolled the vessel might take on a list from which it might not recover. In this photograph the *Passat*'s ballast is being discharged over the side in baskets, one of which can be seen rising from the hold.

Plate 67 (Right)

This fine photograph shows the three-masted iron barque *Bankhall,* built in 1884 at Sunderland, at sea in heavy weather. She has only topsails and staysails set, this being all that might be carried safely in such conditions. In rougher weather than we see here, the staysails might be taken in, leaving only the two lower topsails. These two sails were the minimum required to give the vessel steerage way in strong gales. Should the weather conditions prove too extreme even for this small amount of canvas the vessel could be hove-to with only a minute storm trysail set to keep her from broaching-to; that is, swinging round broadside to the waves where she might easily be swamped or dismasted and founder. This photograph was taken from the *Bankhall*'s bowsprit and shows the full length of the deck, looking aft. Right aft, on the poop, can be seen the silhouetted figure of the helmsman in his customary post at the weather side of the wheel. A weather cloth has been rigged on the rail to give him some protection from the buffetting of the strong wind. The deck seems deserted and the remainder of the watch on deck are probably taking shelter at the break of the forecastle where they will be in earshot if they are called by the watch officer.

95

Plate 68 (Left)

Six members of the crew of the British steel barque *Kilmallie* of 1893 on the main lower topsail yard handing a new sail. Plate 30 shows the crew of the *Port Jackson* bending a new course in anticipation of a change in weather conditions. Here the sail has just been sent aloft using the gantline which can be seen running from a block at the head of the topmast and over the belly of the upper topsail. The sail is still rolled up, just as it was when taken from the sail locker, and the men on the yard will have to spread the head of the sail along the yard and seize it to the jackstay which shows very well in this photograph as a small rail running the length of the top of the yard. Below the yard can be seen the chain sheet of the upper topsail. Some of the gaskets which will be used to lash the furled sail to the yard can just be discerned coiled and hanging from the jackstay.

Plate 69 (Above)

Members of the crew of the Russian (Finnish) barque *Fahrwohl* pose on the mainyard for James Randall's camera, about 1910. The *Fahrwohl* was registered at Åbo (*Turku* in the Finnish language) in the south of Finland at the mouth of the Gulf of Bothnia, but due to the Russian domination of Finland at that time, flew the Russian flag. It is quite likely that the majority of these men are native born Finns, though probably Swedish-speaking, and some of them may even be among those who sailed in the square-rigged ships of the Finnish ship owner Gustaf Erikson as late as the 1930s and '40s when the Åland islands, also at the southern end of the Gulf of Bothnia, became the home port of one of the very last fleets of sailing merchantmen.

The *Fahrwohl* was a medium sized barque of 1,500 gross tons, built by Russell and Company on the Clyde in 1892. Her passages for the first years of the 20th century show a typical pattern of circumnavigatory voyages with common sailing ship cargoes. In 1901 she was outward-bound from Hamburg to the west coast of the USA, for timber or grain. She sailed back to Antwerp to discharge. Her next voyage, in mid-1902, was from the Baltic to South Africa with timber, thence to Argentina and home to Southampton. Early in 1903 she was again outward-bound for South Africa from the Baltic and, after discharging, proceeded to Chile where she loaded nitrates for the Baltic. 1905 saw another voyage to South Africa, continuing to Melbourne to load for Stockholm. A similar voyage was undertaken in 1907, this time discharging in London; then, in 1908, one out to Port Adelaide for a grain cargo for Hull. On October 16 1908 the *Fahrwohl* left Middlesbrough for Fremantle with a mixed cargo of 1,200 tons of phosphate, 670 tons of coke and 400 tons of pig iron. Probably due to shifting of this cargo the barque had to put in to Lisbon with damage to her hull. The cargo was discharged and the *Fahrwohl* returned to Passage West, near Queenstown in Ireland, for permanent repairs. It is possible that this photograph was taken at Passage West at that time. Repairs complete, the *Fahrwohl* moved to Cardiff where she loaded a cargo of coal for Valparaiso, sailing on June 4 1909. She remained under the Russian and, later, after Finland gained her independence, the Finnish flags until 1924 when she was broken up at Wilhelmshaven.

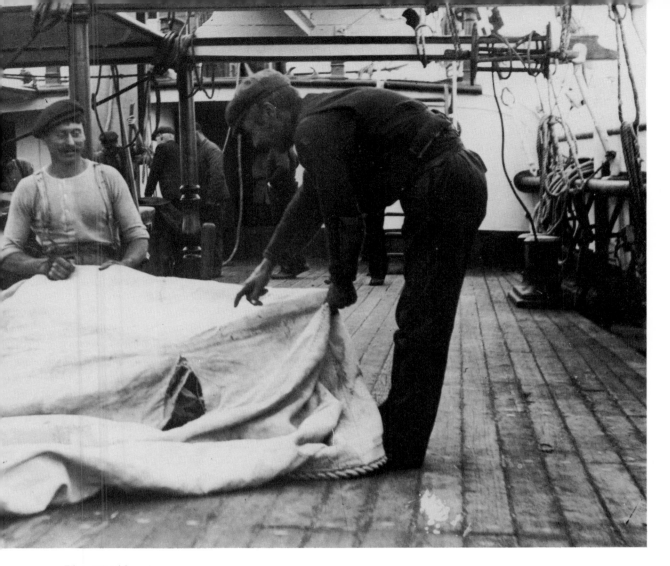

Plate 70 (Above)

The sailmaker and his assistant aboard the barque *Fahrwohl* inspecting weather damage to a sail. Together with the carpenter, the sailmaker was one of the senior hands, almost 'petty officers', aboard a merchant sailing ship. He did not live in the forecastle with the Ordinary and Able Seamen but usually had accommodation in a small deckhouse which would also house his sail loft and, possibly, the carpenter and his workshop. Like the steward of the *Passat* (Plate 56), the sailmaker, carpenter, cook and donkeyman (to look after the donkey engine and steam winches, if they were carried) were known as the 'idlers' aboard ship. This was because they were

day workers and kept no watches. Unless stress of weather required all hands to be called, the 'idlers' were able to sleep through the night, unlike the sailors on watch and watch about who were never able to sleep more than four hours at a time. Constant wear and tear on the sails occurred during a voyage, requiring much repair of the canvas and, frequently, replacement of a sail with a new one, made on board, if a sail blew to ribbons in a heavy gale. In this photograph it seems that a sail has split in a high wind and a new 'cloth' may have to be inserted. Note the substantial bolt-rope around the edge of the sail, providing a strong border and an anchorage for the running gear required to handle it.

Caulking the forecastle head of the three-masted barque *Inverclyde* of 1898. Even the very large steel-hulled vessels of the last days of sail had wood-clad decks and caulking was a routine duty aboard, especially in the hot and sunny fair weather zones of the Tropics. In those regions the deck, despite the efforts of the crew to keep it wet, would dry out and the planking contract. Here and there a seam between the planks would open up and need to be refilled. After first cleaning out the seam, oakum—a mass of oily fibres unpicked from old or condemned ropes—would be rolled into threads between palm and thigh and driven deep into the seam in the deck by means of a caulking iron and mallet. The caulking iron resembles a short, wide-bladed chisel and may be seen in use by the sailor on the left of the photograph. The iron was held usually in the left hand between thumb and forefinger with the palm of the hand turned uppermost. In the photograph the iron is being removed from a deep seam and the seaman appears to be using a heavy caulking mallet known as a 'beetle'. The right-hand sailor holds the more usual form of mallet. A number of seams have been opened in preparation for re-caulking. Once the oakum had been packed tightly between the planks the seams were 'payed' with hot pitch from a long-handled ladle, so completing the seal. When into stormier regions where the decks would remain wet for long periods a ship's planking would again 'take up'; the wood swelling to compress the caulking in the seams, making a thoroughly watertight joint. The forecastle head capstan may be seen on the left of the photograph, with its heavy pawls running in their track on the deck to prevent the capstan running back when under strain. Note also the crew's washing hung to dry on the rail.

100

Plate 72 (Below)

In addition to the requirement that he be able to 'hand, reef and steer', an Able Seaman under sail was expected to have a great many more skills, including those of rigger and, sometimes, sailmaker. Here seamen aboard the French four-masted barque *Champigny* are splicing an eye into each end of a short length of steel wire rope, possibly for use as a stirrup on a footrope. Although wire rope was introduced in the 1830s and had been authorised for use in naval ships by 1838, its use in the merchant service for running rigging purposes did not become common until the development of the square-rigged sailing ship demanded much stronger gear aloft, after the 1860s. The sailor sitting on the capstan is laying up the eye splice at that end of the wire, tucking strands of it back under its standing part to form an eye. Once this is done the eye and splice would be wormed, that is, thick hemp yarn would be laid in between the strands of the wire to present a smoother surface for the parcelling which was laid over it. The parcelling in this case would probably be strips of sacking some two or three inches wide, soaked in linseed or other vegetable oil and wrapped tightly around the wire. Wire rope had a central, hempen core or heart and each strand, wound around the heart, also had a core of hemp. To prevent rot in the hemp it had to be kept lubricated, thus the parcelling would be dipped in oil before it was laid on. Over all this the wire would be served. The serving consisted of hemp yarn again but this time wound tightly over the parcelling, against the lay of the wire, to bind the whole together. The two seamen in the background of this photograph are serving their end of the wire. The left-hand man is using a rigger's screw to clamp together the wire strands while the serving is put on. The whole would then be coated with Stockholm tar to guard against rot.

Plate 73 (Left)

Part of the watch of the full-rigged ship *Iquique* going aloft to furl the main upper topsail on a voyage which took the ship out from London to Cape Town, then in ballast to Sydney where she loaded for London; a return voyage which took the ship around Cape Horn. The *Iquique* left the South West India Dock, London, on May 20 1898 and on board was John Everett, the marine artist, who took this photograph. These were the last days of the British sailing ship and by this time crews were proving difficult to recruit. Steamships offered shorter voyages, better accommodation and food and more pay. Sailing vessels, sadly, became the refuge of the more incompetent seaman or the social misfit—men who were not of sufficiently good quality to gain berths in steamships. This is not to say that there were not top class seamen still serving under sail, for many did remain simply by inclination, but the general trend was downward and the *Iquique* suffered problems with her crew which were rarely encountered in steamers. On the way out to Cape Town a near mutiny occurred amongst the crew which resulted in the Master being knocked down and beaten by one of the watches after he had laid out an insolent seaman. Two of the crew were put in irons and for three nights the officers and Everett, a passenger on board, sat up with loaded revolvers in case of more trouble. When the ship arrived at Cape Town on August 23 the crew was paid off and the men sentenced to 14 days in gaol for their insurrection. A new crew was arranged with a boarding master and was brought out to the ship dead drunk. The seamen were hauled aboard in a bowline and only one was sober enough to stand and go to the mess room. The majority of this crew deserted at Sydney and the Master, in desperation, told one of the local boarding masters to get him a new crew, saying 'I don't care what they are, get hold of anything and put them aboard'. The result was a drugged and drunken crowd of larrikins, some of whom had never set foot on a ship before and yet had good discharges as ABs, (counterfeited by the boarding master), dumped on board and given 24 hours to sober up. By this time the officers had got the ship to sea. One of the shanghaied unfortunates was a disgraced clergyman who was subject to fits and who died shortly after rounding Cape Horn. Another turned out to be a lunatic. In spite of their inexperience, they gave little of the trouble that their predecessors had given and the *Iquique* arrived at London on April 19 1899 without further major incident. On the outward passage from London the crew of the *Iquique* comprised Master and two Mates, three apprentices, carpenter, sailmaker, cook, baker, steward, bosun and 16 men in the forecastle. The sailmaker was over 70 as was one of the ABs, and both had blacked their hair and beards and signed on as 40 years old! It is interesting to note that the sailmaker had in his career been a shipmate with men who claimed to have fought at Trafalgar.

Plate 74 (Overleaf)

The iron ship *Greta* was built at Whitehaven, in Cumbria, in 1874 and here we can see members of her afterguard and crew on the poop posing for the camera, probably whilst the ship was at Port Pirie between October 1885 and January 1886. In the centre of the photograph is Captain William Dickson Cassady in carpet slippers and habitual smoking cap. Captain Cassady was born in 1854 and at the age of only 28 had risen to command of Lowden Edgar's iron barque *Limari*. His Mate aboard the *Limari* was Mr G.W. Garland who followed him into the *Greta*, along with several of the *Limari*'s crew, and who can be seen in this photograph standing to one side of the cabin skylight. Garland had been eight years in the *Limari*, as apprentice, Second Mate and First Mate and after Captain Cassady had left the *Greta* was Master of that ship for nine years. Seated with her daughter Janet at her left shoulder is Mrs Margaret Cassady, the master's wife. At the time that this photograph was taken Mrs Cassady was pregnant and died on the voyage home to England, shortly after her daughter Margaret was born. Not long after Mrs Cassady's death the *Greta* fell in with the ship *Loch Sloy* and her Master's wife, Mrs McLean, took care of the baby. Captain Cassady married again but left the sea in 1891, aged only 37; perhaps he was unwilling to expose his second wife to the risks which had caused the death of his first.

Standing at the wheel is the *Greta*'s Second Mate, Mr Harwood, whilst the young Third Mate, N.M. Petersen, a Dane and probably only lately an apprentice, is seated on the deck next to Mrs

Cassady. Behind Petersen is the ship's carpenter, James Bruce, of Peterhead. Squatting on the saloon scuttle is one of the *Greta*'s Able Seamen, Vincent O'Driscoll, aged 24 and the son of a Northern Ireland coastguard. The lady seated on the skylight and the small boy in the broad-brimmed hat are visitors from ashore.

The *Greta* seems to have been a happy ship under Captain Cassady for she tended to keep her crews. She also made some good passages, once beating the iron clipper *Coriolanus* home from Lyttelton by three days. Cassady seems to have been a most amiable man and, in the nature of many masters in sail, was a great collector of curios. Latterly, in the garden of his house in Laurieston, he had a ship's figurehead—probably that representing the poet Robert Southey from the *Greta* which was broken up at Ardrossan in 1923—and a fully rigged mast. In the *Greta*'s saloon there were ferns and geraniums and a Scots ivy was trained up the interior pillars. A pet dog, no doubt belonging to Cassady, can be seen in the photograph and a bird cage can just be discerned hanging from the spanker boom. Captain Cassady died in 1934.

These men from the *Greta* can be regarded as being very typical of the officers and crews of deep-sea merchant sailing ships before the lure of the steamship drew the majority of more able, dependable seamen away from sail. When this photograph was taken, steam was still establishing itself on world trade routes and the tonnage of sailing vessels on the British register was only slightly less than that of steamships. Of additional note in this photograph are the bales of wool stacked in the shed over Captain Cassady's left shoulder and the very exposed nature of the poop, offering virtually no protection to the helmsman and officer of the watch in bad, stormy weather (see Plate 106).

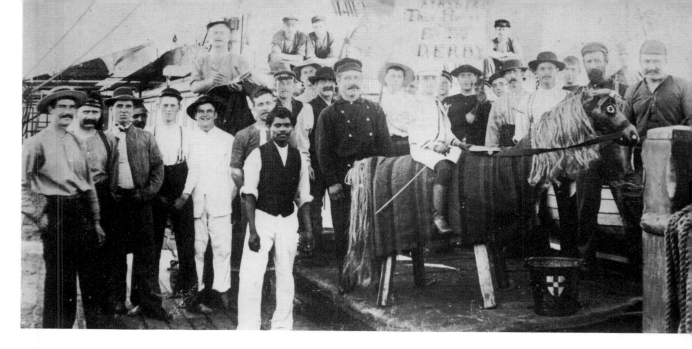

Plate 75 (Left)

The main deck of the famous tea clipper *Cutty Sark,* some time between 1885 and 1895 when she was under Captain Richard Woodget. This group includes, on the right, the *Cutty Sark*'s Chinese cook, Tony Robson. Many years before, a British ship had encountered a small boat or raft, drifting at sea. On investigation it was found to contain a very young Chinese baby—the infant Robson. He was taken aboard and more or less adopted by the British ship's Master and his wife—hence the child's English name. Tony Robson made his career at sea and became a first rate seaman; he was for some time the leading hand aboard the clipper *The Tweed,* under the same ownership as the *Cutty Sark.* In 1885 he joined the *Cutty Sark* as cook, retiring to the galley as did many other fine seamen when age began to make the agile and strenuous life of the men in the forecastle too demanding. He was described as being 'absolutely English in every respect—except his features'.

Plate 76 (Above)

This rare photograph shows the sale of the Dead Horse aboard the British ship *John O'Gaunt* in Latitude 20° South on April 21 1889, whilst on passage from Maryport in Cumbria to Melbourne. It

was common for a shipmaster to allow members of his crew, once signed on, one month's wages in advance to pay for necessary gear and clothing for the voyage ahead. Consequently, for the first four weeks of a voyage much of the crew was working for wages already spent, whilst those who had been shanghaied aboard, and whose one month advance had been paid to the boarding house master by the captain as blood money, were working for nothing at all. It might be expected, therefore, that the men considered themselves to be 'flogging a dead horse' for this month and that the officers might feel similarly about driving a crew to extra effort. Once the month was up and the 'dead horse' worked off, its passing could be celebrated. The crew, aided by the carpenter and sailmaker, would construct a quite elaborate effigy of a horse, as seen here. In a ceremony which involved a special shanty, frequently much speechifying and hilarity, (usually witnessed with some tolerance by the ship's officers), the 'horse' would be hoisted to the lee foreyardarm and, at a suitable climax in the proceedings, dropped into the sea. On those sailing ships which carried passengers it was not unusual to auction off the horse to the highest bidder before its watery interment, thus providing a little pocket money for the crew. The small child astride the horse in this photograph is Thomas Mariner Powles, son of the ship's Master, Captain Thomas Powles. The boy was born aboard the *John O'Gaunt,* at sea.

Plate 77 (Above)

A line of dead albatrosses aboard the barque *Loch Tay*. The dread warning of Coleridge's Ancient Mariner, to whom fell the most calamitous consequences as a result of killing an albatross, seems to have had little weight with the crews of 19th century merchant sailing ships. Although many old shellbacks would profess to believe that the souls of dead sailormen were transmuted into albatrosses and that it was, therefore, unlucky to kill one and a kindness to bring one aboard and let it walk a deck again, this appears to have been little more than paying lip service to an old tradition. The albatross, which is found almost entirely in the southerly latitudes below 40°S, known as the Roaring Forties and Howling Fifties, could quite easily be caught by trailing astern a line baited with a little salt pork. A small hook or triangular piece of bright metal would be put on the line and would become jammed in the bird's hooked beak as it took the bait. Providing the strain on the line was kept constant it was quite easy to pull the huge birds up on to the deck. They did not take kindly to this treatment, however, and quite often became seasick, for although at home on the sea itself they were unaccustomed to the motion of a deck. The large, webbed feet of the birds were quite sensitive, too, and the roughness of the deck would make them bleed. Sometimes the albatrosses were ringed before release, as can be seen in Plate 50, but on many occasions they were killed. This was not for their meat as the merchant seaman was generally conservative about his victuals in spite of his monotonous and savourless diet. More often than not the birds were required simply so that the carpenter could mount their heads as trophies. In November 1913 it was reported by a passenger aboard the barque *Port Jackson* that the carpenter had had so many requests to mount the heads of albatrosses that the quality of his work had declined and the last trophies which he did were not nearly so nice as the first. Sadly, in some cases, the albatross was killed just for sport and aboard the Finnish barque *Lawhill* in 1934 the officers brought them down with a shotgun.

Plate 78 (Below)

Life aboard a merchant sailing ship was demanding and left the crew little time between watches for any sort of recreation. Thus ceremonies such as that which occurred when crossing the Equator were entered into with great enthusiasm. The same feast days that were celebrated ashore were marked aboard ship within the limits set by a monotonous diet and the necessity to work the ship, although rarely were these holidays free from work, as on shore. Music was always popular (singing was used to advantage in the shanties which were sung to coordinate work at the halliards, braces and capstan), and small bands were often formed among the crew. This photograph shows the foo-foo band aboard one of Aitken, Lilburn's sailing vessels. 'Foo-foo' probably originates from the unconventional sound made by an extempore and random collection of instruments. In its battery anything which made a suitably bizarre or strident noise might be included, the eccentricity of the music being matched by that of the attire required of the musicians. The appalling noise made by the foo-foo band and the liberties frequently taken by the musicians were usually taken in good part by the ship's officers.

110

Plate 79

This photograph of some of the crew of the British four-masted ship *Cawdor,* of 1884, shows something of the cosmopolitan nature of ship's crews which was becoming the norm at the end of the 19th century. The *Cawdor* is seen here whilst lying at San Francisco in May 1893 after a voyage of five months from Liverpool. By this time the native-born British seaman was, in the phrase of the die-hard sailing ship seaman, tending to 'leave the sea and go into steam'. That is, to favour service aboard steamships rather than serve under sail. Voyages aboard steamships were shorter than comparable sailing ship passages and conditions of service preferable, for in steamships a sailor had none of the strenuous pully-haul on deck and gymnastics aloft on the yards in all weathers that characterised life aboard a square-rigger. The consequence was that it became increasingly difficult to recruit men for voyages under sail and many foreign seamen, especially North Europeans (who all tended to be 'dutchmen' to the Britons aboard) and sailors from the Latin countries could be found in the forecastles of many British ships. Desertions at ports of call on passage compelled the shipmaster to make up his complement from whatever labour was available locally from the boarding masters and crimps. It is likely that the coloured sailors in this photograph were Americans signed on in San Francisco to replace others who had either signed off or deserted the ship at that port. Coloured seamen have an honoured tradition in both the British merchant shipping industry and the Royal Navy, some being in Nelson's ships at Trafalgar, and black sailors could be found in the gun decks and forecastles of ships both before and after that date—James Wait, the coloured seaman in Conrad's *Nigger of the Narcissus,* is the classic literary example.

111

Plate 80

A group of very typical merchant seamen aboard a merchant sailing ship of the 1890s. These men, probably Able and Ordinary seamen, are posing aboard the steel ship *Glendoon,* of 2,000 tons gross, built in 1894 by A. Rodger and Company, of Port Glasgow, and registered at that port, owned by Sterling and Company. It may be fairly said that during the early part of the 19th century the conditions under which merchant seamen lived and worked were no worse than those enjoyed by many manual workers ashore, particularly in the poorly paid heavy industrial, textile and mining occupations. By the time this photograph was taken, however, the disparity between even the most toilworn longshoreman and the seaman had grown greatly.

Government regulation and unionisation had combined to give the industrial worker ashore a better paid, more comfortable working life than that prevalent during the consolidation of the Industrial Revolution in the early and middle parts of the last century. In comparison these men from the *Glendoon* would have worked for a minimum of 84 hours per week (for that is the result of a two watch system giving a man four hours on duty and four off), and often more during particularly bad weather when all hands were needed on deck. Sometimes a sailing ship might be on passage for three or four months at a time without touching port and, for all that time, each member of her forecastle complement would work watch and watch about with never more than four hours sleep at a stretch; and this without the free Sundays and feast days common ashore. In addition the wage of an Able Seaman, (around £2 15s per month) was low in comparison with that being paid in many industrial occupations ashore.

This was a condition exacerbated by the large numbers of foreign seamen joining British ships in the 1890s, many of whom would have earned less in ships of their own flag. As long as this source of labour was available, British shipowners were unlikely to raise the rate of pay of their seamen to match that of workers ashore. It is true also that, generally, the diet of the factory hand was by this time of a more varied and wholesome nature than that of the seaman.

The Merchant Shipping Act in force when this photograph was taken allowed for the following dietary allotment each day: 1 lb bread (or if bread could not be baked or the flour had become weevily, the equivalent in ship's biscuits), $\frac{1}{8}$ oz tea, $\frac{1}{2}$ oz coffee, 2 oz sugar and three quarts of water plus a daily issue of lime juice as an antiscorbutic. The water allowance was for all purposes, drinking, ablutions and washing of clothes. Ship's biscuits were large and very hard (they were called 'pantiles' by sailors), and could not easily be eaten as they were, but were usually made into 'dandy funk' or 'cracker hash'. The former was made by pounding the biscuits to powder in a canvas bag, whereupon it was mixed with water, jam and fat and given to the cook to bake. The latter was broken biscuits mixed with left-over pea soup, scraps of pork fat, or whatever, and baked in a tin. In addition to the daily allotment there was, for each man, $1\frac{1}{2}$ lb salt beef every other day, alternating with $1\frac{1}{4}$ lb salt pork. $\frac{1}{2}$ lb flour was allowed every other day and $\frac{1}{3}$ pint of peas, again every other day.

These very basic provisions were kept by the cook along with as much of each water ration as he thought he needed and, if he was a good cook, served in as many different ways as ingenuity and a coal-fired range would allow. Additions to this spartan allowance were, in the usual words of the shipping agreement, 'at the Master's option' and might include tinned butter and milk, jam, tinned vegetables and tinned or dried fruit. Plums might be made into duff, a popular dish on Sundays. Oatmeal, if provided, could be made into a porridge, known as 'burgoo', for breakfast. All of these provisions might be served as long as they could be preserved without refrigeration and many of the 'luxury' items had to be bought from the Master, who made a corresponding deduction in the pay due to each man at the end of the voyage. The quality of the salt meat put aboard was dependent to a great extent on the degree of paternalism of the shipowner. It is not surprising, therefore, that on his occasional and brief 'runs ashore' when in port, the merchant seaman was too often eager to indulge himself to the limits of his finances and stamina and make up as much as possible for his gruelling life afloat in a wild and boisterous spree in one of the 'Sailortown' districts of the world's seaports.

The SEAPORTS

Plate 81 (Right) and Plate 82 (Overleaf)

Perhaps the most boisterous run ashore that might be enjoyed by the square-rigger sailor of appropriate inclination was at San Francisco. These two photographs show the city in the mid-part of the second half of the 19th century when it was, perhaps, at its most riproaring. Plate 81, taken in the 1870s, shows the view out across the Golden Gate, the strait used by each ship entering or leaving the superb natural harbour, looking towards the Pacific Ocean. Plate 82 shows the harbour itself and is taken from around California Street looking across towards the notorious quarter known as the Barbary Coast. This area (otherwise, Sydney Town) flourished for four decades and its reputation became common knowledge to every deep-water sailor. The area was infamous as a sink of vice, drunkenness and lawlessness—in one year alone more than 3,000 licenses to serve liquor were issued, an equivalent of one saloon for every 95 persons in the city. Here the seaman might forget the harshness and stringencies of a four or more months' passage out from Europe, around Cape Horn, in a glorious reckless orgy.

If San Francisco was the most dissolute port for the sailor, however, it was probably also the most dangerous, for this was the port best known for its crimping activities. Every ship entering San Francisco was prey to these men who would board vessels even before the anchor was down and sails furled, attempting to entice the crews away for a spree ashore. Their motive was simple. Shipmasters whose crews had deserted could buy men from the crimps and boarding masters. The payment, however, was not made by the shipmaster but was, usually, the value of two months of the seaman's wage, paid in advance and deducted from the sailor's pay at the end of the voyage. This was excused as

payment for the delights in which the sailor had indulged ashore whilst under the crimp's beneficence.

Naturally, it was in the boarding master's interest that his 'guests' should not burden him with a long stay and, since his charges would not be willing to return to sea after only a short time on shore, they were often drugged insensible or made incapably drunk before being dumped unconscious on an outward-bounder. Sometimes these men had been ashore only one night before they awoke, at sea in a ship's forecastle. Usually they had deserted their previous ship, tempted by the crimp, and thus forfeited wages due to them. In San Francisco it had been known for an entire crew to desert a ship at once and from 800 to 1,100 men deserted from British ships annually at that port in the 1890s. Shipmasters were, generally, powerless to resist since they would be refused crew when they were in need of men if they objected to the activities of the crimps.

The revenue from shanghaiing (as the crimp's work was known) at San Francisco could be reckoned in millions of dollars. The most notorious of these men may have been Shanghai Kelly who worked from 33 Pacific Street. He had access beneath his premises by boat and once supplied three ships with crew simultaneously by taking some of his guests on a paddle steamer trip to celebrate his birthday. As they passed out through drinking drugged liquor he put them aboard the ships.

In 1896 the apprentices of the British four-masted barque *Springburn* turned the tables on the crimps with a vengeance when they shanghaiied the equally villainous Shanghai Brown aboard their ship on a winter passage around Cape Horn. Others of these notorious dealers in humanity rejoiced in such

114

colourful names as Calico Jim, Horseshoe Brown and Honest Arnold—no doubt the latter antonymous to the man's character.

It must be said that the accommodation offered by the boarding masters was sometimes preferable to any alternative and that it is difficult to criticise the seaman for wanting to indulge himself after months at sea. In the 1890s, however, an alternative was offered to him at San Francisco for in June 1893 the Seamen's Institute was opened. This seems to have been an immediate success, sometimes up to 400 seamen and apprentices attending concerts held there. Entertainment was provided for ship's crews and, although not of such rollicking a nature as the Bacchanalian alternative, had the effect of more seamen leaving San Francisco in the same ships in which they arrived—and less hard-won pay being left with the shipowner and the crimp. Desertion among ship's apprentices had been running at about 60 per year but began to drop the same month that the Seamen's Institute was opened.

Plate 83 (Left) and Plate 84 (Overleaf)

Sydney, New South Wales, like San Francisco, grew rapidly in the 19th century; much of the impetus for growth stemming from a common cause—the discovery of gold. Between 1850 and 1890 the population of Sydney expanded from 60,000 to 400,000 and the consequent increase in trade and rise in the number of ships visiting the port caused a sailortown district to become established. Plate 83 shows Circular Quay at the head of Sydney Cove in the 1880s or '90s with square-riggers and an Orient Steam Navigation Company liner lying alongside. This quay had been constructed by convicts in the 1830s and '40s and was the last major civil engineering contract undertaken by convict labour in Australia, involving the reclamation of some ten acres of mudflats. In the foreground it can be seen that the gentle curve of the quayside has been straightened to allow construction of ferry piers. On the western side of Sydney Cove, close together, were the Sailor's Home and the Mariner's Church but leading inland from the quay was what has been described as 'the oldest street in Australia', George Street, and here and in the surrounding area were the pubs and other attractions which drew the sailor. The Rocks district, in the bay between Dawe's Point and Miller's Point, was a popular venue for crews from ships at Circular Quay. Among the wilder of the sailor-pubs there were the 'Whaler's Arms', the 'Hero of Waterloo', the 'Sheer Hulk', the 'Labour in Vain' and the 'Sailor's Return'.

Plate 84 shows a busy scene at Sydney at about the same time as the previous photograph. The black-hulled barque at the quay appears to be using her mainyard as a cargo derrick, a common practice when loading or discharging a square-rigger. On the left of the photograph is one of the many buildings which served as warehouses for the cargoes of wool which were to be loaded into the waiting ships and in the bottom right-hand corner can just be discerned a small pile of wool bales.

119

120

Plate 85 (Left) and Plate 86 (Overleaf)

The port of Calcutta lies some 80 miles from the sea on the left bank of the Hooghly River, the port area extending for several miles along the river bank. These photographs were probably taken at some time in the late 1870s or early 1880s and each shows more than a dozen large square-rigged ships lying at moorings in the river. At this time the large majority of cargo shipped from Calcutta was loaded into ships lying in the stream from a huge number of small craft. In the 1880s the Kidderpore Dock was opened for the loading of coal, but the largest proportion of imports and exports were still loaded or discharged over the side. Jute, raw cotton, tea and rice were among Calcutta's exports. Imports included finished cotton and linen goods, hardware and many of the products of industrialised Britain. Calcutta is very susceptible to bore tides occurring throughout the year, the equinoctial ones being most dangerous, and is liable to storms of cataclysmic ferocity betweeen April and November each year, May being a particularly bad month. Cyclones have wreaked great havoc among ships moored in the Hooghly, and it is as a result of a decree issued after a particularly bad cyclone of October 5 1864 when about 200 sea-going craft were set adrift, that ships were required to strike their topgallant yards when a blow was imminent. In Plate 85 it can be seen that nearly all of the ships have sent down their upper yards and have unbent all sail. The method of mooring ships in the Hooghly is also interesting as a further precaution against breaking adrift and can be seen clearly in these photographs. Chain cables emerge from each hawse and are crossed around the ship's stem. A similar arrangement aft held each ship firmly in place in the crowded mooring (see Plate 86). The cables passed under water and were secured to holdfasts, fixed in position by anchors and held above the bed of the river by the large round buoys which show plainly here. It was necessary to employ a diver to shackle the ship's cables in place.

The little brig on the left of Plate 85 may well be one of the pilot vessels of the famous Bengal Pilot Service. The large ship-rigged vessel nearest the camera in the picture here is the *Glengarry* of Liverpool, built at that port by T. Royden and Sons in 1873. Known as 'the clipper of the Indian Ocean' she spent most of her career in the Calcutta trade and was badly dismasted and abandoned in a cyclone off the Sandheads at the mouth of the Hooghly in May 1893, later being condemned.

Plate 87 (Below), Plate 88 (Below right)
and Plate 89 (Overleaf)

One of the most desolate destinations for any 19th century merchant seaman was the west coast of South America. The nitrate-exporting ports of this coast stretched in a chain all down the Chilean coast from Arica in the north to Corral in the south and in the later years of the last century they were, together with the Peruvian guano ports, regular ports of call for square-rigged ships. Plates 87, 88 and 89 show three of these ports, Valparaiso, Coquimbo and Antofagasta.

Wharves, and especially docks, were a rarity in these ports and most nitrate cargoes were loaded from lighters as the vessel lay at anchor. The photograph of Valparaiso (Plate 87) shows a view of the bay with the town in the background. The most notable feature here is the large number of former sailing vessels, unrigged and lying in the harbour doing duty as storage hulks. Inland the ground rises

steeply and lifts now serve the upper areas of the town. In the 19th century this was the district where the sailor ashore would find the entertainment, bars and brothels catering specifically for him. A proper sailor quarter also existed in the lower town and here were the boarding houses and pubs familiar to the merchant seaman in many areas of the world. The pubs at Valparaiso included the 'Shakespere' (sic) and the 'Cross Flags', each of which were run by men who were both crimps and boarding house owners.

The photograph of Coquimbo (Plate 88) shows the harbour as it was late in the 19th century with the Royal Naval store and depot ship HMS *Liffey* on the extreme left and ships lying at anchor awaiting cargoes. Sometimes ships at these ports were at anchor for three months or more discharging, perhaps, a cargo of coal and loading aboard the bags of nitrate. Only the German ships of the Laeisz fleet had an organisation ashore which assured a constant

supply of lighters alongside and a speedy turn round of maybe three weeks. Occasionally these ships would be under sail, leaving the harbour as the last of the cargo was being loaded aboard.

There was little ashore to attract any sailor who might forbear the customary delights of a sailortown and, frequently, shore leave was denied or restricted by shipmasters in an attempt to prevent their crews from indulging in a spree in the town and being lost to them, shanghaied aboard another vessel. Not surprisingly many men, driven by the boredom of 100 days or more in the hot, stifling climate, working coal, ballast or nitrate all day and with little or no shore leave, managed to desert. It was a common sight to see these beachcombers cleaning the streets of the town after they had been rounded up and set to work by the authorities.

The third of these plates, of Antofagasta, (Plate 89) shows more than a dozen big sailing ships lying in the anchorage some distance off the town. Some of

these ships are light in the water, between cargoes, but some are deep loaded, either newly arrived or awaiting the final lighters to top up their homeward cargoes. All along this coast completion of loading and preparation for sailing was accompanied by a ceremony common among ships of all nationalities. As the last bag of nitrate came aboard and before it was stowed in the hold, it would be hoisted up to one of the yards, to the vigorous rendering of a suitable shanty and with one of the crew, usually the youngest apprentice or, sometimes, the heaviest man aboard, sitting astride it. Rockets might be set off and, maybe, coloured lights hung in the rigging as the ship got under way and, to the sound of ship's bells from the other ships in the anchorage, the homeward-bound vessel would make sail. As she passed through the anchored ships each one would be cheered by the crew of the homeward-bounder and, in turn, each ship would respond, cheering the departing vessel and wishing her a speedy passage.

Plate 90 (Above)

This photograph of Queenstown, (the port in Southern Ireland now known as Cobh), was taken in the mid-1860s. More than 20 square-rigged ships, large and small, can be seen lying at anchor in the harbour. The majority of these vessels would not be at Queenstown to discharge their cargoes but simply to receive orders directing them to the particular port at which they were to complete their voyages. It was common for ships to leave their loading ports, perhaps on the other side of the world, with no knowledge of their final destination. The Master's orders would be to proceed to Queenstown, or perhaps Falmouth (both landfall ports for the European continent) and there await instruction.

During the course of a long voyage, sometimes three months in duration, a cargo might be sold several times and, in such cases, not until a vessel arrived in the chops of the English Channel would her discharge port be firmly established. Hence Queenstown became a sort of poste restante with ships calling in for a day or so to collect orders from the agents of the cargo brokers ashore. Even in the very last days almost none of the small remaining fleet of merchant sailing ships carried wireless and the only way to communicate this vital intelligence was by use of these landfall ports or by signals conveyed by means of flag hoists from Lloyd's signal stations strategically placed around the coast of the British Isles.

Plate 91

The port of Liverpool is described by the American novelist Herman Melville in *Redburn,* published in 1849, thus: '. . . of all sea-ports in the world, Liverpool, perhaps, most abounds in all the variety of land-sharks, land-rats, and other vermin, which make the hapless mariner their prey. In the shape of landlords, bar-keepers, clothiers, crimps, and boarding-house loungers, the land-sharks devour him, limb by limb; while the land-rats and mice constantly nibble at his purse'. Yet, he says, '. . . sailors love this Liverpool . . . For in Liverpool they find their Paradise'. And around the thoroughfare of the same optimistically endowed name, Paradise Street, and the surrounding locality, could be found the establishments beloved by Jack-ashore and eager for his money. Here also, offering seamen an alternative to the common lodging house, was the Liverpool Sailors' Home, the foundation stone of which had been laid by Prince Albert on July 31 1846. Although fairly criticised by some for being built to a design closely resembling that of a prison, with galleries, or 'decks', of single 'cabins' around a central well, the Home provided simple but clean and private accommodation for the sailor, who had perhaps returned from a voyage of two or three years spent in a crowded, damp and sometimes squalid forecastle.

This photograph shows the Langton Dock, Liverpool, on April 20 1895 with square-riggers moored bows-on to the quay. It has, unfortunately, not been possible to identify the two vessels on the left of the photograph, both of which are drying sails, but it is likely that they both fly the flags of Baltic countries; the right-hand, deep-loaded barque probably that of Finland, whilst the outermost of the two ships is almost certainly Canadian-built. The two right-hand vessels, each light in the water, had been at Liverpool some months when this photograph was taken. The barque on the extreme right is the *Good Intent,* built at Montrose in 1869. She had arrived at Liverpool from Demerara, possibly with a cargo of sugar, on October 10 1894 after a voyage of precisely two months. The larger barque is the Canadian *Edward D. Jewett,* built in 1871. She had been at Liverpool for a year, having arrived on April 11 1894. On June 18 1895 the *Edward D. Jewett* left for Miramichi in New Brunswick, no doubt for a cargo of timber.

In *Sailortown,* his history of those areas of the world's ports given over to the seaman, Stan Hugill considers Hamburg to be probably the last of the European sailing-ship ports and it seems that the character of its sailor quarter survived longer than most. If this is so then it is consistent with the history of German merchant sail, for Germany, with Finland, was one of the last two countries to have a significant fleet of square-rigged ships in overseas trade. This remarkable photograph of just a corner of the port on the River Elbe was probably taken at some time in the 1870s and shows the harbour so full of sailing ships that no attempt can be made to estimate their number. Indeed, it is interesting to speculate on the difficulties involved in breaking one vessel free from this mass of shipping as each ship in turn became ready for sea.

The district of Hamburg where a sailor could find those diversions in which he could make up in a few days for months of abstinence from drink, women and all delights which could be enjoyed by those with a full pocket, was the St Pauli area, close to the river. As late as 1963 Dr Ronald Hope, Director of the Seafarer's Education Service, writing in *The Shoregoer's Guide to World Ports,* refers to the Reeperbahn, in the St Pauli district, as providing 'strenuous entertainment from sunset to sunrise' and as a street in which 'most tastes are catered for'.

Plate 93 (Overleaf)

This fine photograph shows the South West India Dock, London, crowded with shipping and lighters at a date during the 1880s. We are looking north over the Export and Import Docks which are similarly busy, the masts of ships showing above the low roofs of the dock sheds. Unlike the steamship which is lying alongside the quay in the foreground of this photograph, the sailing vessels are lying head-on with their long bowsprits and jibbooms projecting far over the quayside and sheds. Short piers project from the north side of the dock on to which the ships discharge their cargo, using their yards as cargo booms for there are no cranes on this side of the dock.

A run ashore here took the seaman into what was undoubtedly the toughest part of London at that time and has been described as one of the toughest areas in the world, for the West India Dock gates stood in Limehouse, close to the area popularly known as Chinatown. In the surrounding area, and especially in that strip known as Tiger Bay, enclosed to the north by Cable Street and to the south by the notorious Ratcliff Highway (now St George Street), every temptation would be put before the sailor. Perhaps newly paid off with maybe a year's wages in his pocket and ashore after months of enforced abstinence, the seaman was often more than ready for a spree. If that was the case, and his taste followed the traditional pattern of wine, women and song, then he was well catered for within a short stroll from the dock gates—but at a price, for a very large number of people in this locality lived on the sailor's back, taking from him in a few days and nights what he had taken months to earn. Here were the dives, dance halls, brothels and pubs which depended on sailors from the West India and Millwall Docks, the London Docks and the St Katherine Docks for their livelihood. Some of the more rip-roaring of the public houses, where fights and robbings were common events, are remembered today and have been immortalised in the works of C. Fox Smith and Stan Hugill; the 'Mahogany Bar', the 'Hole in the Wall' and 'Paddy's Goose' being notable examples. The latter, properly called the 'White Swan', was situated in Shadwell High Street and was part pub, part music hall. Since it was frequented by prostitutes it could be said to have provided a full service. Crimps also operated in the area around the West India Docks in the latter part of the 19th century when this photograph was taken.

The merchant seaman was not entirely at the mercy of these land-sharks, however, and pubs could be found where, if the behaviour of the clientele was no less boisterous, at least the sailor got a fair deal. Best known of these is that which still stands at the gate of the West India Docks in West India Dock Road, where the railway crosses. In the last part of the 19th century, this pub, the 'Railway Tavern', became known to seamen the world over through the personality of its landlord, Charlie Brown. In his pub, which now bears Brown's name, the sailor might drink his fill and amuse himself in the dance hall (which can still be seen), without being swindled and robbed as was the case in too many other public houses. Brown was a remarkable man with a generous nature, giving much money to local hospitals. He also kept a museum of nautical curiosities which was added to by sailors returning from deep-sea voyages.

For those seamen newly paid off their ships with no inclination to become embroiled in the wild indulgences available to them or with sufficient will-power to resist a debauch, there were the seamen's homes where reasonable, clean accommodation could be obtained at low cost. In 1835 the Sailor's Home was opened on the site of the old Brunswick Theatre in Well Street (now Ensign Street) adjacent to the site of the Destitute Sailor's Asylum founded eight years earlier by the same management. This home did not close until 1974 by which time it was better known as the Red Ensign Club. Other establishments included the British Sailors' Society home—'Jack's Palace'—in the West India Dock Road.

Sadly, the West India Docks are now closed for Port of London Authority cargo handling operations, as are the London and St Katherine Docks and the Surrey Commercial Docks on the south side of the Thames. At the time of writing only one or two berths at the West India Docks are still working, operated by tenants of the Port of London Authority.

The HAZARDS

Plate 94

Unlike the steamship, which has power to move independently of wind and tide, the sailing vessel was very much at the mercy of those elements. A square-rigged ship at best could manage a course only some 70 degrees from the eye of the wind, though a schooner, especially a small schooner, could do much better. Near the coast close attention by the ship's officers to the speed and direction of the wind and to tidal current and conditions normally allowed sufficient time to avoid a situation in which the ship was set down on to a lee shore. Should wind, current and tide conspire to make such a calamity possible a crew would find themselves engaged in a stiff battle to claw their way out into the safety of the open sea. This vessel, the Norwegian barque *Volo,* built at Arendal in 1891, ran ashore near the mouth of the Bushman's River, Cape of Good Hope, in just such conditions in March 1896. Her port anchor is still aboard indicating that her crew had not time to clear away and drop her anchors in an attempt to prevent her inexorable progress towards the shore.

Navigational error, as well as vagaries of wind and tidal conditions, contributed to many casualties on the west coast of South Africa. A small inaccuracy in a ship's chronometer could, over the period of a long voyage from Europe to the Cape, add up to a considerable discrepancy between ship's time and GMT. The consequence of this could be a misjudgement of a ship's estimated longitude by many miles. A modern vessel has many aids to navigation at its disposal, from simple radio beams from shore stations of which bearings might be taken, to the sophistication of satellite navigation systems fixing a ship's position within yards.

Out of sight of land a sailing ship relied on sextant angles of heavenly bodies for establishing latitude and accurate time keeping for calculating longitude. Following the NE trade winds down the Atlantic to the Equator, the last land that a sailing vessel might see before arriving off the South African coast could be Fernando de Noronha Island or, further south, Trinidad Island, both off the Brazilian coast. South of The Doldrums a ship would bear away into the South East Trades making her easting towards the Cape of Good Hope. Over such a distance, minute navigational errors would multiply and it may be that the cause of the *Volo* running ashore was simply that the South African coast appeared much sooner than expected. Unhappily, the *Volo* became a total wreck, continually pounded by seas much heavier than those in this photograph. The majority of her cargo was salved, however, and sold locally.

137

Plate 95

Collisions between vessels in the busy waterway of the English Channel, particularly at night, were a more common occurrence in the late 19th century than today because, relying entirely on the strength and direction of the wind for their motive power, sailing vessels did not have the independence and manoeuvrability of the steamship. The mighty five-masted ship *Preussen* (Plate 2) was run down and crippled at night in bad November visibility in 1910 by the cross-channel steamer *Brighton* which misjudged the speed of the big square-rigger. Such casualties were quite frequent and the loss of the Swedish four-masted barque *C.B. Pedersen* homeward-bound from Port Germein, in the Spencer Gulf, to the United Kingdom with the cargo of grain and a number of cadets among her crew, at night in April 1937, seems to have been attributable to the same kind of miscalculation of the barque's speed on the part of the steamship which sank her.

On a dark night or in fog a big square-rigger with only oil sidelights and stern light lit (steamships were required to carry a masthead light in addition but the sailing vessel was not allowed to), and with none of the bright electric deck lights with which steamships were being fitted by the 1880s, might be almost invisible to the officers on a steamer's bridge. Neither did the sailing ship carry mechanical fog horns but only feeble, hand-operated apparatus. Consequently there were many casualties involving steamships and sailing vessels.

This photograph shows the port bow of the four-masted barque *Torrisdale*, of 1892, lying in dry dock at Tilbury in June 1909 following a collision with an unknown steamship seven miles west of Dungeness on the night of the 23rd-24th of that month. She was at that time inward-bound from Portland, Oregon, with a cargo of wheat for Hamburg. Following the collision, during which the steamship's stem made this very neat rent in the *Torrisdale*'s bow, the barque was taken in tow by the Dover tug *Lady Crundall* and brought up the Thames to Gravesend. She docked at Tilbury on the afternoon tide of June 25, but only for temporary repairs for she soon left for Hamburg to discharge her cargo and to be drydocked for survey and permanent repairs, which required the renewal of ten plates. Luckily, when the collision occurred the *Torrisdale* was struck forward of her forward bulkhead and the sea was only able to enter and flood the forepeak and not the entire ship, as in the case of the *Berean* (Plate 96).

The *Torrisdale* seems to have been unfortunate at this time for in November 1910 she was again in drydock, this time at Barry, with further damage to her stem and bow plates. Earlier, in September 1903, whilst on a voyage from New York to Sydney, she had undergone a fearful experience when she encountered a succession of terrific gales lasting two days during which she was laid over, causing her cargo to shift. For two hours she was on her beam ends (that is with her masts almost parallel to the sea) whilst heavy seas broke right over her. Cabins were flooded, gear smashed and sails blown to ribbons and for some time no one was able to venture on to the now nearly vertical deck. Once the weather had moderated it took the crew of the barque several days to retrim the cargo and repair damage about the decks and in the rigging. The terror of such a knock-down, the misery endured by her men as the vessel wallows with her masts pointing almost to the horizon and the euphoria of an unexpected reprieve as the ship rights herself are vividly related by Joseph Conrad in Chapter Three of his classic account of the life of a sailing ship crew, *The Nigger of the Narcissus.*

Plate 96

The busy thoroughfare of the Thames was no less a hazardous waterway than the English Channel. Now that so many of the London River docks have closed to shipping and, consequently, little traffic uses the river, it is important to remember that the lower reaches of the Thames were, at the beginning of the 20th century, the entry to the world's busiest port.

In such crowded conditions collisions were inevitable. This photograph shows the Norwegian barque *Berean,* formerly a famous Australian clipper, lying sunk in the lower reaches of the Thames in April 1910. On the afternoon of the 8th of that month the *Berean* was inward-bound from Langesund, Norway, with a cargo of ice (a common cargo from northern latitudes before refrigeration techniques became commonplace) when she was in collision with the German steamship *Julia* of 1,227 tons gross, outward-bound. The *Julia* had just shortly before struck the London County Council sludge vessel *Belvedere* and, no doubt partially out of control, swerved across the river and collided with the *Berean,* striking her on her starboard side amidships. The barque quickly filled and was towed ashore on the north bank below Tilbury Fort by the tug *Simla.* Unlike the majority of steamships which had their engines and boilers placed amidships, so dividing their hold space into separate areas before and abaft the engine space, sailing vessels usually had no subdivision in their holds and the only bulkheads were right forward and right aft. This arrangement had the effect of making these ships little more than huge open boxes. Once the hull between these bulkheads had been fractured and water began to enter the hold there was little that could be done to prevent the ship filling entirely and foundering. The *Berean* was raised the following day and, in tow of the Alexander tugs *Sunbeam* and *Sunshine* again put ashore, this time dry, at Higham Bight. She was later condemned and sold for a hulk (see Plate 19).

140

Plate 97 (Above)

This vessel is the British barque *Formosa,* built by Russell and Co at Port Glasgow in 1883. In the latter part of 1909 and early part of 1910 she was involved in an unfortunate series of accidents which serve as an example of the various natural hazards which might befall a sailing ship. Possibly, at this late stage in the life of the merchant square-rigger, when competent crew were difficult to find and maintenance costs were pared to the minimum, other factors were involved, but nevertheless the separate experiences of the *Formosa* at this time are not atypical—although not usually occurring consecutively.

The *Formosa* left the Tyne on December 26 1909 for San Pedro, California. She anchored in the Downs, probably to await a favourable tide for her passage down Channel, but too close inshore, and on the night of December 30-31 in a fresh westerly wind with misty rain, she went aground. Later the same day the *Formosa* was refloated by the tug *Lady Crundall* which had also assisted the *Torrisdale* some six months earlier (see page 139) and, after divers had surveyed her hull, proceeded on her voyage on January 7 1910. Four days later a strong south-westerly gale blew up and the *Formoa* arrived back in

the Downs in distress and burning blue lights for assistance. She had some sails blown away and an anchor and chain lost. The Walmer and Kingsdown lifeboats were launched and, after taking a tug and slipping her second anchor and chain, the *Formosa* proceeded in tow, with eight lifeboatmen on board, to Gravesend where she was moored to a buoy on January 12. After docking at Tilbury she was back in the Downs again on January 23.

Once more she sailed but on January 29 was yet again in the Downs, this time having put back with her topmasts carried away. Again she was towed up to Gravesend, this time going aground below the Chapman light in the afternoon of January 30. She was refloated the following afternoon but not without the assistance of five tugs. Towed up to Gravesend, she was moored to a buoy, where she is shown in this photograph on February 1 1910 with the Gravesend tug *Victor* alongside. Later she proceeded to the South West India Dock where the damage to her rigging was repaired. It was not until April 9 that the *Formosa* was again ready to resume her voyage, no doubt this time with some trepidation on the part of her crew. She reached San Pedro, five months out, on September 7 1910 without further mishap.

142

Plate 98 (Below)

Some instances of dismasting were not a result of heavy weather carrying the rig away but of the crews being forced to cut away masts in order to save their ship. Here the Norwegian composite barque *Luna,* built at Glasgow in 1868 as the *Guinevere,* is shown lying at Fremantle in 1900 under jury rig after her topmasts had been cut down. The *Luna* had left Table Bay on August 30 1900 on a ballast voyage to Freemantle when, in 39°S 66°E, she encountered winds of hurricane force. Without cargo, and therefore high in the water, the *Luna* heeled over before the wind and the ballast in her hold shifted to one side of the ship, laying her on her beam ends. To free the hull of the weight of its top hamper and help the ship back on to an even keel, the crew climbed out along the almost horizontal masts and cut away the topmasts, upper yards and rigging. No doubt much strenuous work below followed as the crew manhandled the ballast until it was again spread evenly in the bottom of the hold. The hull of the *Luna* was undamaged in this incident and, under a much reduced fore and aft rig, the only square sail being the foresail set from the only yard left crossed, she sailed slowly on for Fremantle where she arrived on October 9. The *Luna* was sold to other Norwegian owners shortly afterwards and rerigged. She was not broken up until late in 1907.

Plate 99

An experienced Able Seaman was expected to incorporate the skills of a rigger in his competence and there are many examples of badly dismasted ships which have made port under jury rig or, in some cases, with the damage to masts and spars made good by the carpenter and crew whilst the ship was on passage. Even in cases of almost total dismasting where very little of the original rig remained, a crew could usually manage to adapt what material remained to set sufficient sail to make a landfall. This photograph shows a scene aboard the American wooden ship *A.G. Ropes,* built at Bath, Maine, in 1884 and one of the last big wooden square-rigged vessels to be launched, dismasted after encountering a severe gale on passage from Hong Kong to Baltimore in 1905. The *A.G. Ropes* left Hong Kong at the end of June that year but limped back to Kobe, in Japan, with most of her rig gone, on July 22. As can be seen in this photograph, her mainmast had been brought down entirely, as had the mizzen; part of the foremast only remaining. On this the crew had managed to contrive sufficient sail to give the vessel way and under this bizarre rig she made port. Although her cargo had been little damaged, repairs to the vessel were estimated at £6,200. Captain Rivers obtained tenders for repairing the *A.G. Ropes* but she was over 20 years old and, at this late stage in the history of sail, had been worth only £5,400 before her dismasting. Lloyds Surveyors recommended designating the vessel a Constructive Total Loss and her cargo was discharged and transhipped. On December 6 1905 the *A.G. Ropes* left Kobe for New York, rerigged as a barquentine. From Anjer, in Java, Captain Rivers wrote that the new rig was working as well as he had expected it to and he hoped to be in New York in four months after stopping at St Helena for fresh provisions. Despite her dusting in the gale the ship was only making about eight inches of water each 24 hours—within the capacity of her pumps. She arrived at New York on May 23 1906 and was handed over to the Luckenbach Transportation and Wrecking Company of New York for use as a towed barge. The photograph clearly shows the deckhouse forecastle which in these later North American wooden vessels provided much better living quarters for the crew than did the forecastles right in the bows customary in too many of the later British ships.

Plate 100 (Left)

This photograph shows the result of a magnificent feat of seamanship aboard the tea clipper *Cutty Sark*, whilst on passage from China to London in 1872. On this voyage the *Cutty Sark* was in company with the crack Aberdeen clipper *Thermopylae* and a fine race seemed to be in prospect when, on August 15 in 34° 26'S 28° 1'E, off the South African coast and in tremendous seas and a gale of wind, the *Cutty Sark*'s rudder broke away from the sternpost. Rather than put into a South African port for repairs, Captain Moodie decided to fabricate a jury rudder on board from the lengths of timber usually reserved for the manufacture of spare yards and masts. The result can be seen in the photograph, which shows the *Cutty Sark* in dry dock after completing her voyage. It must be remembered that all this considerable weight of timber and the chain gear needed to manage it had to be lowered over the side of the ship and fastened in place whilst at sea in heavy weather. Basil Lubbock in *The Log of the Cutty Sark* gives a full account of this remarkable achievement. Suffice it to say that the new rudder was a success and, although it was necessary to restrict the speed of the ship for the remainder of the voyage in order to prevent damage to the makeshift rig, the *Cutty Sark* arrived in London only seven days behind the *Thermopylae*.

Plate 101 (Above right)
One of the hazards which must, undoubtedly, have caused the loss of many ships which disappeared at sea, was a collision with an iceberg. The ship *Garthforce*, shown here moored at Port Natal (Durban) early in 1922, had a very fortunate escape when at 2 am on the night of January 28 1922, in very dark and rainy conditions, she collided with an iceberg in the Southern Ocean southeast of the Cape of Good Hope. In weather thick with rain, sleet or snow, visibility could be very poor. Without the aid of radar a vessel might literally be sailing blind (although it is said that many shipmasters could smell ice from a great distance). Frequently the lookout was unable to see more than a few yards

beyond the bowsprit. In these circumstances many vessels must have sailed straight into icebergs and foundered rapidly as the ice tore open their hulls.

The *Garthforce* was outward-bound from Liverpool to Newcastle, NSW, with a cargo which included rock salt and gunpowder. The repeated impacts with the ice as the ship alternately eased off and struck again caused heavy damage to her bows, the bow plating being rent and buckled from the forecastle deck down to the forefoot, rendering 24 plates beyond repair. Her stem was badly twisted, as can be seen in this photograph, and her fore peak quickly flooded. Luckily, however, in spite of this fearful mauling by the ice her forward bulkhead held and the sea did not gain access to the ship's hold. The bowsprit was torn away, bringing down the fore topmast and main topgallant mast together with their respective yards, causing further damage on deck, and 12 sails were lost or had to be cut away. The crew of the *Garthforce* were quickly at work, however, making all safe aloft and jettisoning 90 tons of gunpowder and some 60 tons of rock salt in order to restore the vessel's trim, as she was then down by the head with the water she had taken aboard.

In this crippled state and with her steering badly

affected by the twisted stem the *Garthforce* was, nevertheless, able to sail 800 miles, limping back to South Africa. During this time two more icebergs were sighted and passed before the ship was met by the Swedish steamship *Unden*, also bound for Australia. After difficulties in connecting a towing hawser, during which the first cable broke in the heavy sea then running, the *Garthforce* arrived at Port Natal on February 20 in tow of the *Unden*. Divers were sent down to examine her bottom but the time was long past when extensive repairs to sailing vessels were economically justifiable and the *Garthforce* was sold for the paltry sum of £500. It appears that she was used as a hulk for a time but spent several years swinging at her mooring, still with her damaged gear aloft. In 1927 it was decided to dispose of the vessel but no suitable berth existed at Durban where she might be broken up. So, after all useful gear had been removed and her hull cut down to within six feet of the waterline, she was towed out and scuttled off Durban on the morning of July 1 1927. We met the *Garthforce* earlier when, in 1898 as the *Iquique* (Plate 73), she was again in trouble in Southern waters, this time with a mutinous crew.

Plate 102

Stress of weather, hurricane force winds, heavy seas and collision were not the only hazards faced by the sailing ship seaman, for sometimes the main danger was from within the ship. Various cargoes, in bulk, could ignite spontaneously and amongst these was coal. Natural heat generated in a coal cargo, or even a ship's bunkers, could rise steadily until a fire resulted, often deep in the ship's hold and difficult to extinguish. Many steamships have arrived in port with little or no damage from a fire which had smouldered sometimes for weeks in their bunkers. Occasionally, however, the situation was more serious.

The ship in this photograph is the Danish iron barque *Lysglimt,* derelict in the Atlantic after a fire in her cargo of coal. On May 1 1921 the *Lysglimt* was in 27°55′N 41°1′W, making her way north in mid-Atlantic on passage from Delagoa Bay in southeast Africa to Christiania (the port now known as Oslo), when it was discovered that her cargo of 2,341 tons of coal was on fire. Three days later it was realised that the fire had gained such a hold that it was not possible for the crew to extinguish it and the barque was abandoned. This action seems to have been prompted, largely, by the appearance of a large four-masted, barque, the *Bellands* of Hull. Confident that the other vessel would heave to and render assistance, the crew of the *Lysglimt* took to the boats, only to see the *Bellands* sail on.

Alan Villiers was aboard the four-master on that trip as an Ordinary Seaman and in his book *The Set of the Sails* reports seeing the *Lysglimt* on fire, still with a few rags of canvas left, the black smoke rising from her hold turning to steam as the unfortunate crew pumped water on to the burning cargo. Much

to the horror of the Second Mate and crew of the *Bellands,* her Captain and Mate refused to investigate the burning vessel and, against all traditions of the sea, left the ship and crew to their fate. So the *Lysglimt* was left by her crew, still burning, with much of the deck and rigging burnt away. Happily her people were picked up by the Italian steamship *Vittorio Veneto* and landed at Dakar.

The master telegraphed the *Lysglimt*'s owners from that port that he was unable to ascertain if the barque had sunk but that he expected her to be 'at the bottom'. The *Lysglimt* had not sunk, however, and on June 17 the master of the steamship *Chezine,* newly arrived at Bordeaux, reported that his ship had fallen in with an abandoned and dismasted vessel on fire between the West Indies and the Azores. A boat had been launched but was not able to approach the vessel as her plates were too hot. It was not possible to ascertain the name of the casualty but there is little doubt that it was the *Lysglimt.* Over a month later a wireless message from the British tanker *Capsa* reported that on July 22, in 30°11½′N 45°20½′W, she had passed a dismasted iron or steel sailing vessel, burnt out. The end of the *Lysglimt* came three days later when crew members from the steamship *Kingsbury* boarded a burnt-out derelict in 30°10′N 45°26′W. No name was found on the vessel, the cargo of which was still smouldering. Since the vessel was an undoubted hazard to navigation, the men from the *Kingsbury* knocked out a number of rivets from the hull and, when it was seen that she was slowly filling, left the barque to founder. This photograph of the *Lysglimt* was taken on May 25 1921, shortly before she began to settle.

Plate 103

In the same way that cargoes of coal were prone to spontaneous ignition, nitrate cargoes could similarly become hotter and hotter until fire broke out. Whereas the remedy with a fire in coal was to pump sea water into the hold, nitrates could absorb water at an alarming rate and the only successful means of extinguishing such a cargo once it was alight was with water which had already had nitrate steeped in it. A quantity of such water was kept in barrels on deck whilst a ship was loading nitrates but, nevertheless, many fires occurred aboard ships lying in those ports on the west coast of South America most noted for this commodity. This photograph shows the British four-masted barque *Reliance* well alight at Iquique in 1901. The *Reliance,* which was built at Liverpool in 1884 and owned by the Liverpool shipowner Charles Corsar, had been at Iquique for some weeks and had loaded 3,200 tons of nitrate when, on September 12, she was found to be on fire. Boats from other ships in the anchorage went to assist and took off the *Reliance*'s crew, but little more could be done. Quickly the fire became out of control and most of the ship's woodwork, sails and rigging burnt away. Later the fore and main masts and mizzen topgallant mast went by the board and fell over the side. In spite of this heavy damage, including decks badly buckled by the heat, much of the *Reliance*'s cargo was considered to be worth salving.

Surprisingly the *Reliance* was not broken up but, after laying idle for a number of years, was sold to Chilean owners who rerigged her and renamed her *Ricart de Soler.* In 1916 she regained her 100A1 class at Lloyds; a tribute to the strength of her iron construction. After undergoing two more changes of name she was broken up in 1924 as the *Antonia Mumbru* under the Spanish flag.

Plate 104 (Below)

On September 19 1911 the Liverpool-registered steel four-masted barque *Sofala,* seen here lying in a South Wales port, awaiting a cargo of coal, left Montevideo bound for Sydney, Australia, in ballast. Little more than a week into her voyage, in a position 33°S 49°W, not far to the north-east of the River Plate, the barque sprang a leak and foundered. The *Sofala* was not a particularly old vessel, having been completed by Russell and Co at Greenock 20 years earlier. The casualty befalling her was simply one of the routine hazards of the sea. Perhaps she had touched the ground in port and set in a plate or, maybe, started a few rivets. A steamship, having divided holds, would most likely have remained afloat but in the *Sofala*'s case the huge, empty hold began to fill faster than the crew could pump out the water. The crew were fortunate for they were picked up by the Norwegian barque *Ingebjorg,* outward-bound from Fredrikshald in Norway, and landed at Buenos Aires. In May 1914 the *Ingebjorg* herself met the same end as the *Sofala* when she was abandoned and deliberately set on fire in the South Atlantic in 33°48′S 49°43′W after being dismasted and heavily battered in a gale whilst on passage from Gulfport to Rosario with timber. It must be remembered that the very large majority of merchant sailing vessels carried no wireless apparatus, only a small number during the last years carrying receiving but not transmitting equipment, and were unable to summon assistance if they got into difficulties. In many cases, if it had not been for the chance appearance on the scene of another vessel, the fate of a large number of sailing vessels in trouble in mid-ocean might never have been known.

Plate 105 (Above)

One of the many vessels which simply disappeared at sea, and of which no trace was ever found of ship or crew, is this four-masted barque *Laurelbank*. She was a product of the same builders as the *Sofala* but was built a year later in 1893. On August 31 1898 she sailed on a ballast voyage which was to have taken her across the Pacific to Portland, Oregon, probably to load a cargo of grain. In October of the same year the ship *Glendoon* (see Plate 80) reported that two vessels, the British barque *Heathfield* which had also left Shanghai on August 31 bound for the west coast of America, and the *Laurelbank,* had encountered a terrific typhoon shortly after sailing. The *Heathfield* put back to Yokohama dismasted, her bulwarks and stanchions badly damaged and her ballast shifted. The *Laurelbank* had, apparently, continued on voyage.

It might have been supposed that the disappearance of the big barque was as a consequence of this typhoon were it not for information given by the American schooner *Prosper*, at Port Townsend after a trans-Pacific voyage from Haiphong. The *Prosper* reported that, on October 28 in a position 34°N 143°30′E, she had sighted a large four-masted barque sailing north-east. The prevailing wind was southerly and it was 'blowing a hurricane'. Some anxiety was now being felt for the *Laurelbank*

and her owners immediately sent a cable to Captain Parry of the British barque *Gifford,* lying at Tacoma, asking him to ascertain whether the *Prosper*'s sighting was indeed of the *Laurelbank*. The reply came back that the description matched but that light winds were encountered some time after the sighting and that if it was the *Laurelbank* that had been seen she would not arrive for a little time yet. Nothing further was ever heard of the ship or her crew and she was posted at Lloyd's as a missing vessel on January 25 1899.

It seems likely that it was the *Laurelbank* that the *Prosper* had seen; the description matched and the vessel was on the course expected of the four-master. But it was blowing hard at the time and, if the *Laurelbank* had not already been lost in the typhoon earlier, she may have foundered in heavy weather shortly after that October sighting.

In the year July 1 1898 to June 30 1899, 22 ships went missing at sea taking with them a total of 279 crew. That year one third of all British sailing vessels were involved in a casualty of some sort. In the 20 years from 1879 to 1899, the total of all British vessels which went missing was 1,153 and the lives of crew so lost was nearly 11,000. This is excluding losses from all other causes. The peak year for disappearances at sea was 1881 when 147 vessels went missing.

Plate 106 (Right) and Plate 107 (Overleaf)

These two photographs give some indication not only of the power of the sea but of how perilous could be the position of the helmsman on a sailing ship in heavy weather, particularly in the Southern Ocean. Unlike his counterpart in a steamship, the bridge of which was usually placed high above the sea amidships and the wheel of which was often enclosed by a wheelhouse which gave protection to the helmsman, the sailing ship seaman steered his ship from the poop deck level and, in British vessels, as opposed to the big American ships (Plate 99) which often had wheelhouses, in the open. In those very large vessels which had their wheels situated amidships (see Plate 60) the hazard was less—the main dangers were the risk of being thrown over the wheel if it kicked or being struck by flying spokes if control was lost, for the connection with the tiller was direct and steering was manual—but vessels steered from the poop exposed the helmsman to even greater perils. Although some British and German ships were fitted with open cabs or whalebacks at the helmsman's back, these offered little real protection from the weather although some from the effects of a big sea breaking over the ship's stern. American vessels had been fitted with wheelhouses for some time and, latterly, these were occasionally heated which greatly improved the helmsman's efficiency. Partly sheltered accommodation for the helmsman was also commonplace in British coasting and long-voyage schooners. But generally in big British sailing vessels the completely open steering position was favoured until well into the 20th century.

Every so often a sea, bigger than its predecessors, would build up. If the stern of the ship rose to this wave and it passed harmlessly beneath the ship then no damage occurred, but if the ship, in the trough of the foregoing sea, could not rise in time the giant might break aboard. The 1,538-ton steel barque *Meinwen* (Plate 106) was so 'pooped' in 1904 whilst on a voyage from Liverpool to Australia. She had left Liverpool on October 1, crossed the Line within a month and reached the meridian of the Cape of Good Hope in 54 days. It was in 42°30′S 76°30′E, halfway between South Africa and Australia, that the incident occurred. There was a fresh westerly wind blowing and the Master, Captain Potter, had just gone to breakfast at 8 am when a great sea, estimated at 35 ft in height, towered over the stern and crashed aboard. The end of the cabin skylight burst and the cabin immediately flooded, sending the Master rushing to the deck. He found the ship broached-to and the main deck full of water. The wheel had been smashed by the sea, the wheel box had gone and the standard compass was knocked over. The Mate had cuts about the face and had lost two teeth. The two helmsmen had been washed forward and were both severely bruised and disabled. Four other members of the crew had wounds that needed dressing.

Below, the water had inundated the lazarette and rendered most of the dry stores in it useless. Under the circumstances the *Meinwen* was fortunate, for other vessels, out of control and broached-to after a pooping, had foundered and there are incidents of several men together being washed overboard by a huge sea coming aboard. The photograph shows the subsequent temporary repairs made by the crew to the *Meinwen*'s wheel. The bare steering mechanism shows where the wheel box or steering locker was washed away. Temporary tackles were rigged to the tiller and the barque was able to proceed, arriving at Melbourne on December 26. Damages to the ship were estimated at £500.

Plate 107 shows the poop of the iron ship *Orealla*, built at Liverpool in 1882, after a big sea had come aboard. As can be seen, the wheel was almost completely destroyed and has had to be rebuilt using lengths of timber roughly cut to shape. The binnacle has disappeared completely. In addition to this it can be seen that a length of her poop rail has been torn away and replaced with a temporary structure. This damage extended down to the main deck where a section of solid bulwark on the port side was smashed by the sea.

The weak spots of any ship's hull were the hatches. Should a sea manage to break or wash away the hatch covers and so flood the hold, a ship might rapidly be overcome by hundreds of tons of water pouring below. No pumps could hope to cope with a sudden innundation of this nature and many sinkings can be attributed to this cause. On board most vessels, when entering southern latitudes, extra heavy timbers were lashed across the hatchways to reinforce the hatchcovers and guard against this hazard.

The DECLINE OF MERCHANT SAIL

Plate 108 (Overleaf)

We have discussed in earlier sections of this book the problems which owners of latter day sailing vessels encountered in paring their costs to the minimum in order to remain competitive, and the difficulties of recruiting crew of sufficiently good quality to man their ship. One answer was to dispense with as much square sail as was possible, thus reducing the initial cost of a ship's outfit and diminishing the number of crew required to manage the sails. This vessel, the barquentine *Westfield,* and her four sisters *Oberon, Titania, Renfield* and *South of Jura,* were an attempt to combine efficiency with low running costs.

The *Westfield* was built, as were all her sisters, by Russell and Company of Port Glasgow, the series beginning in October 1893 with the completion of the *Oberon.* The last of the five to be completed was the *Westfield* in March 1896. Comparison with earlier photographs in this book, particularly that of the *Formosa* in Plate 97, a slightly larger barque of 1883 and also a product of Russell, will show that the *Westfield*'s hull is no different from a barque-rigged vessel.

An unusual feature of the *Westfield* was her 'midships deep tank for water ballast. 40 ft long and with a capacity of 480 tons, this tank when full dispensed with the need to take solid 'stiffening' into the hold when empty of cargo with all the attendant costs of the process. Of most interest in the *Westfield*'s rig are the small booms fixed to the caps of the main and mizzen lower masts. These are to carry the clews of the triangular topsails over the triatic stay, (which runs between the heads of the main, mizzen and jigger lower masts, giving mutual support to each mast), so abolishing the need to go aloft and pass the sheets and tacks of the topsails over the stay as the vessel came about—as was normally done in big schooners and barquentines. Reference to the photograph clarifies this. Extra sail could be set from the yards seen on the main and mizzen masts. From these some of the five sister ships could set a three-cornered topsail and a small lower sail which was set on one side of the yard—whichever was most appropriate for the direction of wind—and hauled across to the other as necessary. With this rig it was claimed that 'the sail area was considerably in excess of an ordinary barque of the same tonnage'. These barquentines, and others like them, seem to have been a success, a crucial factor being that the fore-and-aft sails, set from gaffs and booms, should be kept small enough to be manageable by a small crew and avoid excessive wear on the canvas. The huge four-masted barquentinne *Mozart,* built in 1904 and carrying what were probably the largest gaff and boom sails ever set in any vessel, gave endless trouble to her crews taking in and resetting the gaffsails to avoid expensive wear in adverse conditions of weather and sea. She was financially successful, but had she been a five-master, setting the same sail area but in smaller sails on more masts, much of this would have been avoided.

The *Westfield* was retained by her original owners, J. Nicoll and Company, until 1921 when she was sold to Italian buyers and renamed *Felicina.* She was wrecked two years later. She and vessels like her had pointed the way for the further development of the big merchant sailing vessel, had not the development of world trade rendered such vessels uncompetitive, however economically they were operated.

Plate 109 (Below)

During the latter part of the 19th century and early 20th century the standard merchant sailing vessel engaged on long deep-sea voyages became the big four-masted barque of some 2,000 tons gross or more—double the size of the average large merchantman of 30 years or so earlier. At the same time, as has been explained, for reasons associated with the need for economy and the difficulties encountered in recruiting suitable men, these larger ships were being sailed with smaller and smaller crews. The gear of the huge steel barques was much heavier than anything previously fitted to square-rigged ships and the labour involved in bracing 18 yards to meet a change in the wind or to bring a ship on to the other tack, might tax the members of a small watch severely.

This photograph shows an ingenious solution to much of this toil and perhaps the most successful application of labour-saving devices to the square-rigged ship. At the top of the photograph can be seen the foot of a mast and immediately abaft it the big fly wheels and crankshaft of the ship's pumps; these are standard fittings. In the centre and foreground of the photograph, however, are mechanical brace and halliard winches, designed to ease the backbreaking task of hoisting and swinging the enormous yards. The two halliard winches, for raising the upper topsail and upper topgallant yards, can be seen in the foreground. With the use of these much of the

arduous work at the capstan was avoided.

More interesting, though, is the brace winch in the centre of the photograph. This is designed to brace simultaneously the lower yard and both topsail yards on the mast which it serves, paying out on one side and taking in on the other. It can be seen that the winch consists, in essence, of three parallel shafts each fitted with two tapering drums. Each shaft serves one yard. The brace from the port yardarm is led to the port drum and that from the starboard yardarm to the starboard drum. As the winch is turned (by means of cranks on the upper, single shaft), one drum takes in on its wire brace, thus pulling round the yard while the other pays out, so allowing the yard to swing. The drums are tapered to allow for the varying rates at which the wire runs during the movement of the yard, so keeping all taut. By means of the winch a minimum of two men could brace all three of the heavier yards on a mast—a job which would employ the whole watch on a ship without brace winches.

The brace winch was invented by Captain J.C.B. Jarvis and first tried out in the ship *Duntrune* of which Jarvis was master in the first half of the 1890s. Although they were a success Jarvis had to fit them at his own expense, not only in the *Duntrune* but in each ship he commanded subsequently. He had them fitted in the *Lawhill* (see Plate 23) when he had a big four-master at the turn of the century, and was able to run her with a crew of only 18 men. In spite of the benefit of these devices, as demonstrated by Jarvis, they were rarely fitted in British or American ships, being viewed with suspicion by shipowners, but were taken up by German shipowners, particularly F. Laeisz, and used extensively in the big German nitrate carriers. This photograph was taken aboard the *Passat,* formerly a Laeisz vessel (see Plate 52). Due to a flaw in the patent rights, Jarvis did not benefit much financially from his invention but there can be little doubt that the success of both the German Laeisz fleet and Erikson's fleet of sailing vessels under the Finnish flag is due, partly, to the contribution of economy made possible by the use of these devices.

Plate 110 (Overleaf)

Along with the more familiar bulk cargoes, such as grain, coal, nitrates and metal ores, which were proving to be the staple of the sailing ship in her latter years, increasing quantities of oil began to be carried in square-rigged ships from the end of the 19th century. The idea of carrying bulk oil in sailing vessels was not a new one, a pioneer sailing tanker being the iron ship *Ramsey,* built on the Isle of Man in 1863, having a capacity of some 1,400 tons of petroleum. Much oil was carried in barrerls aboard sailing ships but this was wasteful of cargo space while the barrels themselves accounted for much of the vessel's deadweight.

The vessel in this photograph is one of the large fleet of sailing tankers owned by the Anglo-American Oil Company of London, the four-masted barque *Brilliant.* At the time of her completion in May 1901 the *Brilliant* was the largest sailing vessel on the British register, measuring 3,765 tons gross. She began by carrying case-oil, that is oil in thousands of small, separate cans, but in 1909 she and her sister ship the *Daylight* were adapted at New York for the carriage of oil in bulk, extra plating being added in the 'tween decks to provide a space in which the oil cargoes could expand or contract according to the climate. Very soon afterwards the *Brilliant* came under the ownership of the Tank Storage & Carriage Co Ltd and in July 1914 was sold to the 'Flying P' line of F. Laeisz at Hamburg. She was renamed *Perkeo* at New York but on her first homeward voyage to Hamburg was arrested in the English Channel by the Royal Navy and taken to Dover, for by this time the First World War had broken out. The *Perkeo* was transferred to the Norwegian flag as the *Bell* and was torpedoed and sunk west of the Scilly Islands on a voyage from Portland, Oregon to the Channel in March 1916. Increasing demand for oil in the period immediately preceding World War 1 had begun to render the carriage of bulk oil under sail obsolete and by the end of the war the trade had largely died out. In 1918 the Anglo-American Oil Company had only one pure sailing vessel, the *Calcutta,* in its fleet.

Plate 111 (Right) and Plate 112 (Overleaf)

An example of a big square-rigged ship with an auxiliary engine has been seen already when the five-masted barque *France* of 1912 was discussed (Plate 22). Here in Plates 111 and 112 are two more examples, one earlier than the *France,* one later. The first photo shows the *R.C. Rickmers,* also a five-masted barque, built at the owner's shipyard at Bremerhaven in 1906. This vessel is only slightly smaller than the *France,* (which it will be remembered was the largest sailing vessel ever built), measuring 5,548 tons gross. Her deadweight capacity was in the order of 8,000 tons. The *R.C. Rickmers* was not intended for use as a cargo-carrying cadet ship, although she did fulfil this role on one occasion, but was to complement her owner's Far East cargo service which was operated with a mixed fleet of steam and sailing vessels. Her engine was a conventional triple-expansion unit of 125 Nominal Horse Power—all that might be found in many steamships of only 1,000 tons gross—although it was said to give the big barque a not unrespectable speed of seven knots when loaded and eight knots in ballast. The funnel above her engine room can be seen, with its associated ventilators, between the mizzen and jigger masts. Several successful passages were made by the *R.C. Rickmers,* usually without much contribution from her engine, and she appears to have acquitted herself well under sail. In August 1914, whilst at Cardiff loading a cargo of coal for Valparaiso, the barque was requisitioned by the Admiralty and placed under the British flag, being renamed *Neath.* On March 27 1917 she was torpedoed without warning by a German submarine 28 miles South by East from the Fastnet and foundered, her Master being taken prisoner.

Plate 112 shows an interesting view of the stern and counter of the German four-masted auxiliary barque *Magdalene Vinnen* whilst in dry dock. This vessel was built in 1921 at Kiel as a training ship to engage in the trade between Europe and the west coast of South America. She was smaller than the *R.C. Rickmers,* being of 3,476 tons gross, and was built on the 'three island' design with a poop 41 ft long, a bridge deck (to accommodate her cadets) of 107 ft and a 27-ft forecastle. When not under sail she was propelled by an oil engine of 128 Nominal Horse Power, slightly more powerful than the steam engine of the larger *R.C. Rickmers.* The screw can be seen clearly in this photograph. On deck she was fitted with brace and halliard winches to each mast and a number of motor winches in addition. In 1936 the *Magdalene Vinnen* was bought by the Norddeutscher Lloyd who renamed her *Kommodore Johnsen* and employed her in the Australian grain trade, carrying cadets as before. After World War 2 she passed to the Russian flag and was renamed *Sedov.*

It must the said, as has been stated in relation to the *France,* that with a few notable exceptions working in special conditions, auxiliary engines were not a success in big deep-water square-rigged sailing ships. They were only of any significant use in port at the beginning and end of each voyage. Whilst on voyage an engine could only be used in times of calm, or following wind, for the large amount of windage inherent in the masts, yards and rigging of a sailing vessel made it difficult for the small engines to push the vessel along against even a slight head wind. Generally these auxiliaries were under-powered. An engine of sufficient power to propel the vessel at a useful speed virtually turned the ship into a fully powered motor vessel or steamship, making the sailing rig redundant. Extra crew were needed to operate and maintain an engine and, in the case of steam-powered vessels, to stoke boilers. The very long poop deck of the *R.C. Rickmers,* measuring 180 ft in length and evident in the photogtraph, is an indication of the crew space required for these extra hands who, whilst the ship was on passage under sail, would be superfluous. It is significant to note that the greatest of the German sailing ship fleets, that of F. Laeisz, did not include one auxiliary vessel.

Plate 113 (Below)

The five-masted auxiliary schooner *General Serret,* seen here at a mooring in Dover harbour drying her sails soon after the First World War, was one of a large group of sisters built during the war not as a means of competing with conventional powered vessels, but as a matter of short term economics. These vessels were part of the enormous resurrection of the sailing vessel which took place during and after the First World War and which led to the construction of at least 800 big schooners, 30 or more big square-rigged vessels and a number of smaller vessels.

Loss of vessels due to enemy action, debilitation of European shipyards occasioned by transfer of personnel to the fighting services and shortage of steel, together with a great maritime boom, all combined to produce a shortage of shipping towards the end of the First World War. Many big schooners were launched from New England yards. Shipyards on the American north-west coast, surrounded by the great pine forests and specialising in wooden vessels, were also in a strong competitive position. The demand for large four- and five-masted schooners increased rapidly and fortunes were made with this class of tonnage.

In 1917 Andre Tardieu, French High Commissioner for War, was sent to the United States to negotiate the construction of 200 wooden auxiliary transport schooners. The *General Serret* was one of more than 40 of these vessels completed for the French. All told, 99 of these big five-masters, not all with auxiliary engines, were built on the West Coast, some passing to Norwegian and later to Finnish owners.

The schooner in this photograph was built by the Foundation Shipbuilding Company of Portland, Oregon, in 1918 and measured 2,117 tons gross. She was fitted with twin triple-expansion steam engines of 68 Nominal Horse Power, driving twin screws, and had twin funnels arranged athwartships. For a few years such vessels were very profitable, but the wartime boom was shortlived and in the ensuing slump the big wooden schooners could not compete with triple-expansion-engined steam vessels. Nevertheless, a number of them survived in trade at sea into the Second World War and comprised one of the western world's two last fleets of big sailing vessels, the other being the fleet of square-rigged ships owned in the Åland Islands.

Plate 114 (Above)

Also an example of wartime output from the Oregon shipyards during World War 1, this unlovely vessel is the six-masted schooner *Fort Laramie,* built at North Bend, Coos Bay, in 1919. The straight stem with its plain knee, the square-sectioned hull with slab sides and little sheer all contribute to her appearance of hasty construction occasioned by a shortage of tonnage during the First World War. During the 1914-18 boom three six-masted schooners, similar to the *Fort Laramie,* were built on the west coast of the USA, together with a remarkable 99 five-masters, 56 four-masters and eight big three-masters.

In the same period on the East Coast ten five-masters and 133 four-masters were built. In eastern Canada 323 schooners were launched. Most of these vessels were much better looking than the unfortunate *Fort Laramie* and numbered among them were some fine and long-lived schooners.

Plate 115 (Above right)

We have seen already the large German four-masted auxiliary barque *Magdalene Vinnen,* built by Krupp at Kiel in 1921 (Plate 112). Here is another auxiliary built by the same shipbuilders for the same owners a year later. This vessel is the *Werner Vinnen,* one of five sisters all built by Krupp in 1922 and all carrying the same unusual rig. The others in the quintet were the *Adolf Vinnen, Carl Vinnen, Christel Vinnen* and *Susanne Vinnen.* All five were, basically, conventional schooners but equipped, uniquely perhaps amongst schooners, with yards on both the fore and mizzen masts. In the photograph the *Werner Vinnen* has the gaffs of her large fore-and-aft sails lowered to the deck, almost out of sight and shrouded with canvas covers. This rig, combining elements of both square and fore-and-aft rigs, was envisaged as developing the maximum efficiency and driving power commensurate with economy of gear and crew. The *Carl Vinnen* had

only four ABs and one OS in each watch. The auxiliary engine of the *Werner Vinnen,* in common with those fitted in her sisters, was a four-cylinder motor of 97 Nominal Horse Power, and said to be an unused submarine engine. Each of these vessels was built for the Vinnen service to the River Plate, although some were employed occasionally in the grain trade between Australia and Europe; the *Werner Vinnen* coming home from Adelaide to Dungeness in 137 days in 1923 and the *Carl Vinnen* in 125 days from Albany, Western Australia, to Hamburg in 1926. On the whole it would appear that these handsome vessels were financially successful.

During the 1930s two of these schooners were converted to motorships relying entirely on new, more powerful engines for propulsion, their rig being removed. These were the *Christel Vinnen* and the *Werner Vinnen,* which was also lengthened at the same time. Both were lost in 1944, the *Christel*

Vinnen north of the East Frisian Island of Juist on March 29 and the *Werner Vinnen* two months later in the River Elbe in May 1944. The *Adolf Vinnen* had been lost very early in her career when she stranded beneath Lloyd's Signal Station at the Lizard on the afternoon of February 9 1923 whilst on passage from Kiel to Barry, and went to pieces under the action of the sea. Only two of the sisters survived World War 2. The *Carl Vinnen* was laid up at Carthagena, Spain, during the conflict, passing to British control after the war. On August 31 1952 she arrived at Hamburg to be broken up. The *Susanne Vinnen* lasted until 1975, having been re-engined in both 1947 and 1954, at which earlier date she lost her rig. She had been sold to Italians in the early 1930s and remained under the Italian flag, subsequently bearing the names *Patria, Imperatore, Patria* once more, *Ernesto S.* and *Piombino.* She was broken up in Italy during the first quarter of 1975.

169

Plate 116
This four-masted barque, the *Padua,* was the last big, square-rigged merchant sailing ship to be built, being completed at Wesermunde in Germany in 1926 at which time, significantly, she cost more to construct than a conventional steamship of the same deadweight tonnage. The *Padua* was owned by F. Laeisz and Company and was built for the nitrate trade between Europe and the west coast of South America, but was employed also in the carriage of grain from Australia. Accommodation was provided for 40 cadets. The addition of the *Padua* brought the number of big sailing ships in the Laeisz fleet to seven—all four-masted barques except for the *Pinnas* which was ship-rigged. By the outbreak of war in 1939 this number had reduced to two: the *Padua* and the slightly larger four-master *Priwall,* a contributory factor to this decline being the development of synthetic nitrates after World War 1. In the interim Gustaf Erikson had bought the *Pamir* and *Passat,* and the *Parma* had also hoisted the Finnish flag under the management of Captain Ruben de Cloux, with Erikson a substantial shareholder. In 1932 the *Peking* was sold to become the stationary schoolship *Arethusa* on the River Medway (see Plate 123). The *Pinnas* had been abandoned, dismasted off the Chilean coast in 1929. During the war the Chileans seized the *Priwall,* renaming her *Lautaro.* Under her new name she was used as a cargo-carrying sail training ship by the Chilean Navy and was lost by fire in March 1945 when a cargo of nitrate she was carrying ignited. Only the *Padua* remained German when hostilities ceased. Together with the Norddeutscher Lloyd training ship *Kommodore Johnsen,* ex-*Magdalene Vinnen* (see Plate 112), which was renamed *Sedov,* the *Padua* was allocated to Russia as part of war reparations. She was renamed *Krusenstern* and is now to be seen occasionally taking part in international races of sail training ships, an interesting sight amongst the more usual purpose-built training ships which have never earnt their living as cargo carriers.

172

Plate 117 (Left) and Plate 118 (Overleaf)

A great boost was given to the construction of large steel merchant sailing vessels in France at the turn of the century by a system of government subsidies designed to encourage and regulate a stable merchant service. Begun in 1881, these subsidies extended not only to construction of new vessels but were granted as relief on operating costs. At first a building subsidy of 60 Francs per ton gross for iron and steel ships was paid, in addition to a grant of 1½ Francs for each net register ton per 1,000 miles sailed. The latter reduced gradually as the ships aged. In 1893 the subsidy on building was amended to 65 Francs per ton gross and the operating subsidy altered to 1 Franc, 70 Centimes, allowed to each ton gross rather than net. This particular amendment had a curious effect on the appearance of the ships themselves.

It will be recalled from an earlier discussion of gross and net register tonnage (Plates 18, 19 and 20) that each of these figures represents an expression of a ship's internal volume and that the former represents the entire ship, including so-called 'non-earning' spaces. Since the operating subsidy was paid on each gross register ton it was in the shipowner's interest to increase this figure as far as was practicable. Plate 117 shows one of the vessels which has taken advantage of this ruling. She is the ship *Amiral Cecille,* built at Rouen in 1902. Of 2,847 tons gross this vessel had a length of 283 ft. Clearly evident in the photograph is the unusual length of her poop deck, measuring 136 ft in length; a feature more commonly expected of training ships carrying large crews. Many of the 'bounty ships' built under the government subsidy scheme had this feature, some having only very short well-decks separating poop from forecastle and a few being entirely flush decked. Naturally, the more accommodation provided, the greater was the tonnage of the ship and the greater would be the subsidy paid on each voyage.

The bounty not only benefited the French shipowner financially but gave his ships greater independence in seeking cargoes. Whilst an unsubsidised British ship might have to lie at anchor in a foreign port, sometimes for weeks, awaiting a cargo, the Frenchman could afford to weigh anchor and spend time sailing in ballast to a port where a cargo might be more readily available. Ballast voyages wasted ship's time, crew's wages and victuals and were without profit, but at the beginning of the 20th century French sailing vessels were able to spend three-fifths of their round voyage in ballast without financial loss, being buffered against such loss by the bounty.

The maiden voyage of the *Amiral Cecille* took her outwards from Cardiff in June 1902 to Table Bay, thence to Poro on the French Pacific island of New Caledonia where she loaded nickel ore for Rotterdam, this cargo being a staple for French sailing ships. The Cardiff to Table Bay leg of the voyage was probably with coal, Table Bay to Poro most probably in ballast.

The growth of the French sailing fleet over a period when the number of large British sailing vessels was declining was remarkable. In 1886, five years after the introduction of the bounty system, there were only 57 sizeable iron and steel sailing vessels, totalling 40,000 tons net, under the French flag. By 1902, the last year that any large sailing ships were built in France, this number had risen to 253 ships and the net tonnage had risen by ten times. Comparable British figures of similar ships over this period show a decrease in numbers of vessels from 1,750 to 1,088 and a decline in tonnage from 2¼ million to 1½ million tons. The subsidies had very largely ceased before the First World War and the slump which followed it rendered the large number of French ships and barques remaining unprofitable. In the early 1920s they began to be laid up in large numbers. Plate 118 shows the scene on the Canal de la Martiniere at Nantes at that time. There are 18 square-rigged ships in this photograph, all laid up awaiting employment which was never to come. Gradually, one by one over a period of years, they left their berths and were towed away to be broken up. The *Amiral Cecille* arrived here in August 1921. In January 1925 she caught fire and was burnt out.

173

Ålandsfartyg på redden

Plate 119

This is Mariehamn, the only town of the Åland group of islands which lie in the Baltic at the entrance to the Gulf of Bothnia, at a date in the early 1930s. During the period between the First and Second World Wars this fine, unspoilt harbour, otherwise of small significance internationally, became the home of the last of the world's fleets of deep-sea square-rigged sailing ships, principally under the ownership of Gustaf Erikson. Usually he was able to acquire vessels for little more than their scrap value and in 1936, a little after the time that this photograph was taken, owned a remarkable total of ten four-masted barques, six three-masted barques, two full-rigged ships, four schooners and a barquentine, in addition to two motor vessels.

A great tradition of manning, management and the maintenance of sailing ships in the Åland Islands contributed much to Erikson's success and his big square-riggers fitted well into the contemporary social and economic background of the islands. Additionally it must be borne in mind that Erikson's capital outlay was small and, in comparison with that of a line of steamships, his maintenance and crew expenses were low. He carried those bulk cargoes (principally grain and timber) already described as the staple of the latter day sailing ship, where speed of delivery was not of the essence. Erikson's fleet was a financial success which made possible the foundation of a line of motorships now comprising more than 20 vessels. This modern fleet includes not only general cargo carriers but vessels offering refrigerated cargo space, container and paper carriers and a ship with roll-on, roll-off capability. Modern Erikson ships operate throughout the world, serving the Baltic, Continental and Mediterranean ports, North America including the Great Lakes, and ports of Africa, the Pacific and Far East.

The Erikson vessels in this photograph are the *Archibald Russell* (nearest the camera), then from left to right, *L'Avenir, Olivebank, Viking* and the barquentine *Mozart,* owned by Hugo Lundqvist. The vessel in the distance is the *Winterhude.* The four-masted barque *Pommern,* latterly under the Erikson flag, is now preserved at Mariehamn as a memorial to sail, the Erikson fleet, and the unique position of Mariehamn in the days of the Last Tall Ships. She is the world's finest surviving big merchant sailing ship.

Plate 120

This little barque, the *Janes,* built by Iliff, Mounsey & Company at Sunderland in 1868 as the *Charlotte,* was destined to become the last square-rigged merchant vessel (apart from the native-built craft of the Indian sub-continent) in deep-sea trade under the British flag. In 1907 the *Charlotte* became the *Tomaso Drago* under the Italian flag, passing to the Swedish flag in 1912 as the *Janes.* In 1924 she was re-registered at Port Louis, Mauritius, as the *Diego* and hoisted the Red Ensign. For some years she traded in the Indian Ocean but on August 16 1935 was reported in Lloyd's List as being overdue. Nothing more was heard of the barque until early in September of that year when the owners of the British steamship *Clan Macphee* received a message from the steamer's Master dated September 3 reporting that the *Diego* had been wrecked on Eagle Island in the Chagos Archipelago on June 20. Luckily the crew of the barque and the passengers she had on board had all survived their prolonged period as castaways and were taken, aboard the *Clan Macphee,* to Peros Banhos, close to Eagle Island in the same central Indian Ocean group.

So the last British square-rigger employed on ocean passages was gone. But the *Diego* was only nominally British, being registered at Port Louis. The last voyage undertaken with cargo by a large, steel square-rigged sailing vessel registered at a United Kingdom home port had ended in 1927 when the full-rigged ship *William Mitchell* arrived at Ostend from Tocopilla and was sold to German shipbreakers for £2,100. The wooden barquentine *Waterwitch* of Fowey, built as a brig at Poole in 1871 and employed in the home trade, was the very last square-rigged merchant vessel to work from a home port in the United Kingdom. In 1936 the *Waterwitch* was laid up at Par, in Cornwall, and in 1939 was sold to owners in Tallinn, Estonia, for further trading.

JANES.

179

Plate 121 (Below)

It is a curious, but nevertheless appropriate, accident that the very last of the big steel square-rigged merchant sailing ships to carry cargoes should have been named *Omega*, but so it was and here she is lying at moorings awaiting a cargo whilst under the German flag. Originally the *Drumcliff*, one of Gillison & Chadwick's famous 'Drums', this vessel was built by Russell and Company at Greenock, being completed early in 1887. She joined a fleet of ten more iron sailing ships of which four others were four-masters. During the 1890s Gillison & Chadwick began to add steamships to their fleet and dispose of their sailing vessels. In 1898 the *Drumcliff* was sold to the Rhederei Aktiengesellschaft von 1896 under whose ownership she received her prophetic second, and last, name. For 16 years the *Omega* traded with her running mates in a fleet which, just before the First World War, numbered more than 20 square-riggers. On August 1 1914 she arrived at Callao, three months out from Hamburg, to load a cargo of nitrate. Three days later Great Britain declared war on Germany and the First

World War began. The *Omega* was interned at Callao for the duration of the war and, following Germany's defeat, was taken over by the Peruvian Government. She was adapted to accommodate a number of cadets and sailed for some years as a cargo-carrying cadet ship. In the mid-1920s the *Omega* came under the ownership of the Compania Administradora del Guano, also of Peru, with whom she was to remain until her loss. For many years the *Omega* operated on the South American west coast, running cargoes from the guano islands to mainland ports in company with the barque *Tellus*, built in Rotterdam in 1891 as the *Evertsen,* and the ship *Maipo*, built in Germany for N.H.P. Schuldt in 1893, but finally only the *Omega* was left—the last big merchant square-rigger left in trade. On June 26 1958, whilst on a voyage from the Pachacamac Islands a little to the south of Callao to Huacho, a distance of a little more than 100 miles, with 3,000 tons of guano in her hold, the *Omega* sank. Probably the old hull, built over 70 years previously, sprang a leak.

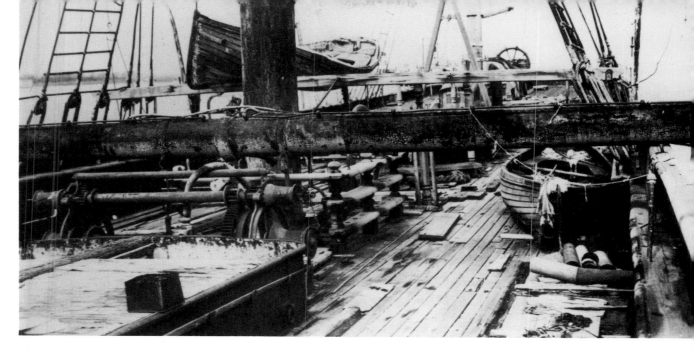

Plate 122 (Above)

A poignant and melancholy photograph from the last days of merchant sail but showing an incident atypical of that which befell the large majority of square-riggers. This scene of desolation and decay was taken aboard the Italian iron barque *Maria Madre* which lay anchored at Paysandu on the River Uruguay throughout the first quarter of the 20th century. She was completed by R. Dixon and Company at Middlesbrough in 1875 as the *Langland* for W.H. Tucker and Company of Swansea. Until 1897 she was owned at that port, making voyages to the west coast of South America, probably with cargoes of coal outwards and copper ore homewards, then hoisted the Italian flag under the ownership of Bartolomeo Balestrino, who seems to have been her Master as well as owner. In April 1902 the *Maria Madre* was chartered to load a cargo of salted hides at Paysandu, for Antwerp. Loading was completed by July 1902 but a dispute arose between the barque's Master and the shippers of the cargo which resulted in the Master refusing to sail. After four months of deadlock the cargo was landed and found to have deteriorated somewhat during the time that it had been aboard and further claims were lodged against the ship's owner by the owner of the cargo. Eventually the Uruguayan government stepped in and arrested the barque, whereupon the crew became difficult and attempted to prevent government

officials boarding the ship by laying the Italian flag on the gangway! Consequently the fractious crew were taken ashore—only to refuse to reboard when asked to do so. All this time the Uruguayan government continued to uphold the claims against the Master of the *Maria Madre*.

Meanwhile years passed and the barque's gear became so rotten that it was necessary to gradually dismantle the ship. This photograph shows the main deck in 1926—24 years after the dispute arose. It can be seen that the mainyard has been lowered and rests on the port and starboard rails; the starboard boat has rotted and collapsed on its chocks and the decking, without any maintenance, has warped and split. At one point the vessel was rigged right down to lower masts and main topmast. In 1929 the dispute was at last settled but by this time, of course, the ship was totally unfit for sea. That she was still afloat after 27 years is a testimonial to the resilience and endurance of an iron hull. In fact her hull was in such good condition that the *Maria Madre* was not immediately broken up but, in 1936, sold for conversion to a nautical club at Buenos Aires.

Although not a common occurence, the experience of the *Maria Madre* is mirrored in other incidents, particularly those of the Uruguayan barques *Clavo* and *Pavo* which lay at their moorings at Montevideo in a state of neglect for many years in the 1920s and '30s after being arrested for debt.

Plate 123

If the previous photograph strikes a note of sad nostalgia, this one of the four-masted barque *Peking* of 1911, might be said to provide a somewhat happier conclusion to the story of the deep-sea merchant sailing ship. The photograph of the *Maria Madre* shows the final stage of merchant sail as decrepitude and dissolution; this one of the *Peking* shows, to some extent, regeneration and a renewal of interest in the sailing ship. Although, at the time of writing, none of the visionary plans to reintroduce sail, in the light of increasing fuel oil costs, to the world's sea lanes has yet reached fulfilment, there are a number of Victorian and later square-rigged merchantmen in different states of preservation throughout the world to remind us of the contribution which wind-propelled ships have made to developed, industrialised society. Foremost among these is, of course, the *Cutty Sark* at Greenwich, the only fully rigged, composite-construction, clipper ship to survive, saved by the far sighted and public spirited Captain W.H. Dowman (Plate 28) who bought her from her Portuguese owners for preservation. America has the *Star of Finland,* the *Balclutha,* the *Falls of Clyde* and the *Wavertree,* among others, whilst in Sweden is the *Viking* and the *AF Chapman,* in Finland the *Sigyn* and in Germany the *Passat.* All these vessels have been altered in various ways from their trading days. Remaining in the most original and authentic condition of them all, at Mariehamn in the Åland Islands, is the *Pommern.* Among the square-riggers preserved in other countries is the *Polly Woodside* in Australia.

The *Peking,* originally a Laeisz nitrate carrier, was sold in the 1930s to the Shaftesbury Homes and *Arethusa* Training Ship at Upnor on the River Medway to become a stationary training ship. In 1974 the hulk *Arethusa* (as the *Peking* then was) was bought by the South Street Seaport Museum of New York and towed across the Atlantic with the intention of re-rigging the vessel as she was when under Laeisz ownership, though this has not been achieved. In this photograph she is seen in Green & Silley Weir's dry dock at Blackwall on the River Thames, undergoing preparation for the tow, on March 13 1975.

It has been said, with a good deal of justification, that a big ship so preserved, out of her element and with smartly painted hull and neat decks crowded with visitors, can convey nothing of the workmanlike urgency and atmosphere that she would have had in trade, with men in her forecastle and bustle about her decks, or at sea in heavy weather when the ship lived in, and responded to, every change in wind or sea. A sailing ship in dry dock or moored to a quay, some say, is a passive creature belying her nature, from which one can learn little of the way of the ship or her men at sea in the compulsion of sea trade. Much of this is true; to be aboard a dead ship in dock cannot help us to true understanding of the hardships, hazards and attractions of the life of a seaman in sail.

But it would not, presumably, be claimed that a visit to a mediaeval castle or the site of some early activity of the Industrial Revolution was without value and educational worth. Imagination and perception are vital assets in such visits, and it is no different with historic ships. No more than we would consider demolishing the shells of Beaumaris Castle or Rievaulx Abbey should we think of breaking up the hulls of the unrigged clipper *Carrick* at Glasgow or that of the now partially restored steamship *Great Britain* at Bristol. By careful appreciation and imaginative interpretation of these monuments of our industrial past we can gain a greater understanding of the part played by sea trade in the development of modern society and the contribution made by generations of men who took to, or were compelled to adopt, the demanding, dangerous yet sometimes rewarding trade of seaman under sail.

List of plates and
National Maritime Museum negative numbers

Plate No	Neg No	Plate No	Neg No	Plate No	Neg No
1	P3332	42	P7166	83	C5041
2	A8760(b)	43	P4789	84	NPA Coll.
3	G2362	44	P8259	85	A9707(u)
4	P8188	45	P8223	86	C4876
5	4606	46	P8236	87	C5043
6	P2729	47	P8242	88	C5044
7	G2367	48	P8251	89	NPA Coll.
8	P2626	49	P8272	90	A527/45
9	P3310	50	P8256	91	G3609
10	Hill 576	51	P8241	92	5896
11	4603	52	P486	93	P618
12	C2259	53	P8277	94	P6686
13	C4513	54	P8444	95	G852
14	P3814	55	P8350	96	G873
15	4790	56	P8321	97	G567
16	G1554	57	P8435	98	P4528
17	8454	58	P8457	99	P7114
18	P2409	59	P8462	100	7794
19	P1804	60	P8485	101	P3245
20	P3390	61	P8502	102	P4552
21	P137	62	P8499	103	P5715
22	P3148	63	6009	104	P6075
23	P4331	64	6125	105	P4302
24	P2337	65	P7246	106	P7307
25	P2390	66	P8509	107	P7315
26	P7396	67	P7122	108	G2375
27	G1781	68	P7267	109	P8452
28	A1660	69	P7145	110	G2360
29	A3105	70	P7144	111	P5573
30	C4434	71	P7255	112	P4595
31	C4444	72	P7131	113	P286
32	C4426	73	Everett Coll.	114	P3119
33	C4419	74	6562	115	P6798
34	C4420	75	7802	116	P5219
35	C4438	76	P7263	117	P1423
36	P7217	77	P7283	118	NPA Coll.
37	P7155	78	P7398	119	C605/1
38	P7194	79	C5055	120	P3967
39	P7173	80	P7223	121	P5155
40	P7181	81	C4384	122	P7301
41	P7177	82	C5037	123	B8832/8A